Improving Nutrition as a Development Priority

Addressing Undernutrition in National Policy Processes in Sub-Saharan Africa

Todd Benson

RESEARCH REPORT 156

INTERNATIONAL FOOD
POLICY RESEARCH INSTITUTE
sustainable solutions for ending hunger and poverty

IFPRI®

International Food Policy Research Institute
2033 K Street, NW
Washington, D.C. 20006-1002, U.S.A.
Telephone +1-202-862-5600
www.ifpri.org

DOI: 10.2499/9780896291652RR156

Library of Congress Cataloging-in-Publication Data

Benson, Todd David.
Improving nutrition as a development priority : addressing undernutrition within
national policy processes in Sub-Saharan Africa / Todd Benson.
    p.   cm.—(IFPRI research report ; 156)
  Includes bibliographical references.
  ISBN 978-0-89629-165-2 (alk. paper)
  1. Nutrition policy—Africa, Sub-Saharan.   2. Food supply—Africa, Sub-
Saharan.   I. Title.   II. Title: Addressing undernutrition within national policy
processes in Sub-Saharan Africa.   III. Series: Research report (International Food
Policy Research Institute) ; 156.
TX360.A357B45   2008
363.8′5610967—dc22   2007048412

Contents

Tables

Figures

Boxes

Foreword

Undernutrition has, fortunately, risen on the policy agenda in Africa in recent years. In 2004, an international IFPRI 2020 conference held in Kampala on food and nutrition security in Africa drew attention to the issue, and high-level policymakers noted the problem and the need for action much more than they had before. Still, undernutrition remains a fundamental challenge to achieving improved human welfare and economic growth in Sub-Saharan Africa. To address that challenge, national governments must undertake appropriate policies and actions. Politically, however, a high prevalence of undernutrition is not seen as anomalous and indicative of the inability of governments to fulfill their duties to their citizens.

This report examines the findings from a qualitative institutional study in Ghana, Mozambique, Nigeria, and Uganda to determine what it is about national-level policymaking, nutrition, and the issue of nutrition in policymaking circles that makes it difficult for governments to target undernutrition as a national development priority. The underlying determinants of improved nutritional status fall across several sectors. Consequently, much more so than for most other development challenges, the routine operations of government through sector-specific action are unlikely to succeed in comprehensively eliminating undernutrition.

Given this poor fit between nutrition and government operations and the consequent problems for establishing leadership on the issue of undernutrition within government, the absence of effective nutrition advocacy coalitions in all of the study countries turns out to be a key constraint to building national commitment to overcoming undernutrition. As such, there is little demand to hold government agencies in each sector accountable for assisting the undernourished. Although the challenge of building advocacy efforts should not be minimized, this study suggests several actions that advocacy coalitions can take to raise the profile of undernutrition as a national development problem.

This report provides guidance on how national governments can be encouraged to address the needs of the undernourished so that such individuals can enjoy long, healthy, productive, and creative lives. It suggests that development actors continually highlight for political and bureaucratic decisionmakers the fundamental constraint that undernutrition poses to achieving key development objectives, including economic growth and poverty reduction. Moreover, it should be made clear that governments can support the implementation of relatively low-cost solutions that enable all to meet their nutritional needs.

Undernutrition is a solvable problem that requires public action and commitment. IFPRI is committed to the task of comprehensively eliminating undernutrition globally and will continue to examine the policy processes through which such public action can be fostered and maintained.

Joachim von Braun
Director General, IFPRI

Acknowledgments

The research from which this report draws was conducted under a grant from the United States Agency for International Development (USAID) to the International Center for Research on Women and the International Food Policy Research Institute (IFPRI) for the project "Promoting Agriculture and Nutrition Strategies to Reduce Hunger and Under-nutrition" (agreement no. 2789-001-43-01). The initial research was an institutional study that focused on the barriers to and opportunities for linking the agriculture and nutrition sectors to reduce undernutrition in Uganda, Mozambique, Nigeria, and Ghana. The report builds on insights gained in this earlier study. The opinions expressed herein do not necessarily reflect the views of USAID or the International Center for Research on Women.

Tammy Palmer, Robin Satcher, and Charlotte Johnson-Welch made important contributions to the fieldwork and initial writeup of the research. The fieldwork for the research was made possible through the assistance offered by members of the project teams in Ghana (led by Rosanna Agble), Mozambique (led by Manuel Amane), Uganda (led by John Aluma and Joyce Kikafunda), and Nigeria (led by Bussie Maziya-Dixon and Isaac Akinyele). Cheryl Jackson coordinated support from USAID. This document has benefited from the insights of Kathleen Kurz, Kerry MacQuarrie, Simel Esim, John Anderson, Carole Douglis, and Marc Cohen, as well as from extensive comments provided by an IFPRI internal peer reviewer. I am grateful to them all.

Acronyms and Abbreviations

BASICS	Basic Support for Institutionalizing Child Survival (Nigeria)
GDP	gross domestic product
GPRS	Ghana Poverty Reduction Strategy
HIPC	highly indebted poor country
HIV/AIDS	human immunodeficiency virus/acquired immunodeficiency syndrome
IFPRI	International Food Policy Research Institute
MADER	Ministry of Agriculture and Rural Development (Mozambique)
MDG	Millennium Development Goal
NCFN	National Committee on Food and Nutrition (Nigeria)
NEEDS	National Economic Empowerment and Development Strategy (Nigeria)
NGO	nongovernmental organization
NPC	National Planning Commission (Nigeria)
PARPA	Plano de Acção para a Redução da Pobreza Absoluta [Action Plan for the Reduction of Absolute Poverty] (Mozambique)
PEAP	Poverty Eradication Action Plan (Uganda)
PMA	Plan for the Modernization of Agriculture (Uganda)
PPP	purchasing power parity
PRSP	Poverty Reduction Strategy Paper
SETSAN	Secretariado Técnico de Segurança Alimentar e Nutrição [Technical Secretariat for Food Security and Nutrition] (Mozambique)
TANA	The Agriculture–Nutrition Advantage project
UFNC	Uganda Food and Nutrition Council
UNICEF	United Nations Children's Fund
USAID	United States Agency for International Development
WIAD	Women in Agricultural Development Directorate (Ghana)

Summary

Undernutrition remains one of Sub-Saharan Africa's most fundamental challenges to human welfare and economic growth. Both for normative and instrumental reasons related to human and economic development, a strong case can be made for the importance of addressing the needs of the undernourished as an issue of public concern and, hence, the desirability of governments to prioritize and make substantial investments in efforts to reduce undernutrition among their citizens. The policies and actions of national governments are a critical component in enabling individuals and households to achieve nutrition security. Central government has the responsibility for establishing institutions and infrastructure and providing resources without which many of the poor, in particular, will remain undernourished. Yet in most nations in Sub-Saharan Africa, a high prevalence of undernutrition in the population is not seen as anomalous or indicative of the inability of the government to fulfill its duties to its citizens. Undernutrition tends to be treated in national policy processes as a business-as-usual issue. There is no drama associated with it; no perception that the issue is critical to the future of the country, the continued political success of government, or to the well-being of its citizens. As a consequence, there is low political demand for action against undernutrition, and most governments in Sub-Saharan Africa do very little to ensure that nutrition-related goods and services are provided to their citizens. This problem is at the center of this report.

This report examines the findings from a qualitative institutional study in Ghana, Mozambique, Nigeria, and Uganda that investigated what it is about national policymaking, nutrition, and nutrition in policymaking that makes it difficult for undernutrition to be targeted as a national development priority. Much more so than for most other development challenges, the routine operations of government through sector-specific actions are unlikely to lead to success in comprehensively eliminating undernutrition. A conceptual framework of the determinants of nutritional status is examined from the perspective of policymaking and the institutional organization of government to assess the various opportunities for and constraints on prioritizing action to address undernutrition in the public sector in these countries. In each country, four interrelated elements of the policy processes related to addressing undernutrition are examined. The first three elements are interdependent—policymaking structures, including both formal institutions and less formal political interests; political actors who engage strategically with particular policy processes; and the narrative or persuasive understanding of undernutrition that is the basis on which choices are made to derive policy in this area. However, by themselves these three elements do not explain policy change. A fourth element, timing, is also critical. The presentation of the study findings in each of the four countries is organized using these elements of the policy process.

Although the four study countries provide some useful contrasts in their policy processes, administrative organization, and levels of economic and political development, the dominant commonality is that none of the countries has effectively prioritized undernutrition in the objectives and resource allocation patterns of government. The following points summarize several of the most important country-level findings of the study.

- In all four countries, undernutrition is generally seen as part of the context within which government works as best it can. High levels of undernutrition do not threaten the legitimacy of the governments of these four countries or invoke a sense of crisis. When addressing undernutrition, the governments tend to focus on bureaucratic arrangements and programming that involves mid-level managers rather than political leaders, with little attention to the issue in any fundamental policy reforms in which they may engage. As a consequence, all four countries consistently underinvest in efforts to reduce undernutrition. Such an approach is maintained even when evidence shows, as in Ghana, that levels of child undernutrition have increased in recent years.

- In all four countries, there is a limited understanding among political leaders and policymakers of both the costs of aggregate undernutrition in the country for national development and the determinants of nutritional status. This failure is evident in the limited linking of any policy narratives on undernutrition to master development narratives in the country.

- In the face of the awkward institutional location of nutrition in government, the governments of Mozambique, Nigeria, and Uganda have developed formal food security and nutrition policies and established food security and nutrition coordination bodies. However, the record of success of these policies and agencies in shifting government resource allocations toward addressing undernutrition is quite poor. There are several reasons why they tend not to be effective. Perhaps most salient is that sectoral ministries in government tend to view themselves as being in competition with one another for resources. Most participants in the budgeting process assume that resources allocated to another sector are lost to their own. Policies and coordinating agencies that have cross-sectoral scope do not fit this sectoral pattern of resource allocation and add a layer of complexity to it.

- Existing sectoral mandates tend to be used to determine what public actions are undertaken to address undernutrition and to assign responsibility for carrying them out. Yet in all of the study countries for all the sectors concerned, whether health, education, agriculture, water and sanitation, or others, nutrition activities tend to be viewed as secondary priorities and improved nutrition outcomes as secondary sectoral objectives.

- The actors who are directly involved with nutrition advocacy and the coordination of nutrition activities present some common patterns across the countries. International partners tend to be important in nutrition-focused activities and their coordination. This situation is especially the case in Mozambique, but can be seen in all of the countries. On the other hand, there is seemingly little engagement by national civil society groups in nutrition advocacy. This failure likely reflects a combination of a lack of attention to engaging existing civil society groups on this issue and a lack of public awareness of the costs of undernutrition and how to address the problem.

- The study countries differ in the level of expertise that they have in addressing problems of nutrition. Mozambique has very few professional nutritionists, whereas Nigeria has many hundreds of them. However, there is little evidence that the prospects for the undernourished in Nigeria are any better than in Mozambique. The manner in which available human capacity in nutrition is used is certainly as important as the presence of trained nutritionists. Moreover, where policymaking is centralized and relatively ordered, a few motivated nutritionists are adequate to provide policymakers with necessary nutrition analyses and technical inputs to guide the formulation of policy and the allocation of resources. However, where policymaking is decentralized and develops in a bottom-up manner, as is the ambition in Uganda, the constraints on human capacity in nutrition are much broader. For local governments to take action to address the needs of the undernourished among their citizens, they must be provided with considerably more information on the costs of the problem at the community and subcounty level and what needs to be done to reduce it. For this effort, local governments need more technical support from nutritionists.

With between one-quarter and one-third of all children in these countries stunted in their physical growth and cognitive development, the human costs of undernutrition are immense. Although small positive steps can be identified in all four countries, none of the governments has succeeded in putting in place policy mechanisms to reduce sustainably the numbers of the undernourished in their populations. Certainly, none has effectively prioritized undernutrition in its policy objectives and allocations of resources.

In part, this failure is due to the poor fit of undernutrition as a public policy problem in the sectoral organization of government. The underlying determinants of improved nutritional status fall across several sectors, including health and agriculture. Given this poor fit and the consequent problems for establishing leadership on the issue of undernutrition in government, national advocacy coalitions should be formed around the issue. The absence of effective nutrition advocacy coalitions in the study countries appears to be an important constraint on building the commitment of government to assist the undernourished attain nutrition security. Yet the creation of such coalitions is problematic. To some degree, leadership for and participation in such advocacy efforts depends on the personal qualities of the participants. However, if established, there are several actions that such coalitions should take:

- Consistently link nutrition policy narratives to those of the master development framework for the country. The problem of undernutrition should be couched within a framework that demonstrates to a country's leaders how their master development objectives are not likely to be attained if the constraints imposed by undernutrition on needed development are not removed.
- Make sure that the government continues to recognize its duty to ensure that its citizens are properly nourished. Normative reasons for addressing undernutrition are compelling.
- Make it clear to senior government leaders that improving nutrition requires a broader set of action across multiple sectors than those needed to attain food security. Cultivate policy champions, particularly senior political and bureaucratic decisionmakers. This is particularly important in countries with more disordered and personalized policy processes, such as Nigeria.
- Raise the awareness of the general public of the burden that undernutrition imposes on their well-being and what can be done effectively to reduce this burden. While it is useful in its own right to increase understanding of the importance of good nutrition and what constitutes good nutritional care, doing so also provides a foundation for political dialogue centered on the problem of undernutrition at more local levels. Over time, such efforts will increase expectations on government that it has a responsibility for ensuring that all citizens are properly nourished.

Advocates for nutrition must present clear and consistent messages of the roles that the government and sectors within it should play in reducing undernutrition in a concerted and harmonized manner. The objective is that government agencies will recognize the important contributions that they can make to assist the undernourished and to build a sense of responsibility on the part of government for seeing that these contributions are made across all of the sectors concerned.

The perception of undernutrition as being part of the normal order of things must be altered. Advocacy groups should generate a perception of crisis related to undernutrition to foster significant, urgent, high-profile action by government. Although such a qualitative change in the perception of nutritional conditions cannot be sustained in the long term, at least incremental changes in the profile of the policy problem can be exploited so that more effective actions are taken to assist the undernourished. Because undernutrition is a solvable problem that, in part, requires public action to address sustainably, governments should and can be held accountable for the persistence of undernourished women and children in the population, the unnecessary suffering they experience, and the limited potential they have to live long, healthy, productive, and creative lives.

CHAPTER 1

Introduction

Undernutrition remains a fundamental challenge to improved human welfare and economic growth in the developing world. Because of profound poverty, low food availability, poor health services, unhealthy environments, and lack of knowledge on appropriate nutritional care, about one-sixth of the population of the developing world—more than 800 million people—are undernourished (FAO 2005). This undernutrition poses a relentless obstacle to the economic development of many developing countries. The continuing human costs of shortened lives characterized by illness and reduced physical and mental capabilities are enormous. The aggregate costs at national levels impose a heavy burden on efforts to foster sustained economic growth and improved general welfare when so many individuals, because of undernutrition, are unable to attain their full social and economic potential and contribute creatively to their own and their nation's economic well-being.

The problem is particularly severe for most countries in Sub-Saharan Africa. In contrast to most other regions of the globe, the numbers of undernourished in this region have actually increased by nearly 20 percent since the early 1990s. Almost 40 percent of children in Sub-Saharan Africa are stunted in their growth and must face a range of physical and cognitive challenges not experienced by their better-nourished peers (UNICEF 2005). Undernutrition is the major risk factor underlying more than 28 percent of all deaths in Africa—some 2.9 million deaths annually (Ezzati et al. 2003). Because of this level of undernutrition, the countries in the region are unlikely to attain the many national and international economic development and poverty reduction goals formulated in recent years.

The policies and actions of national governments are a critical component in reducing undernutrition and enabling households to achieve nutrition security. If a government accepts that it has some responsibility for promoting the social and economic welfare of its citizens, among its duties will be the provision of institutions, infrastructure, and resources to its citizens—most notably health services, clean water, sanitation, education, and reliable access to food—without which many households, particularly poor ones, will remain undernourished. Yet even when confronted with large numbers of the undernourished in their populations, many governments of developing countries do not place the achievement of nutrition security among their key development priorities. Few governments, both in Africa and elsewhere in the developing world, sustainably allocate significant state resources to combat undernutrition. As a consequence, few of these governments have been successful in assisting the many undernourished in their populations to meet their nutritional needs. This disparity between the high prevalence of undernutrition in many African countries and the relatively low level of public resources allocated to address the problem motivates the inquiry described in this report.

Objective

To gain insights into why undernutrition is problematic as an issue of public concern in many African states, this report examines the findings of a qualitative institutional study on nutrition in four countries in Sub-Saharan Africa—Ghana, Mozambique, Nigeria, and Uganda. The focus is twofold. First, a general understanding is sought on why it is difficult for undernutrition to be targeted as a national development priority. Consequently, I draw on a conceptual framework of the determinants of nutritional status and examine it from the perspective of policymaking and government organization to assess the opportunities for and constraints on prioritizing action to address undernutrition within the public sectors in these countries.

Second, I look in more detail in each country at four interrelated elements of the policy processes that are relevant to addressing undernutrition. The first three elements are interdependent—policymaking structures, including both formal institutions and less formal political interests; political actors who engage strategically with the process for particular policies; and the narrative or persuasive understanding of undernutrition that forms the basis for policy choices in this area (Keeley and Scoones 1999). However, they alone do not explain policy change. A fourth element, the timing of policy change, is also critical. The presentation of the findings of the study in each of the four countries is organized using these elements of the policy process. In the final chapter of this report, these same elements will then be used to assess how advocates might engage strategically in policy processes at the national level in Sub-Saharan Africa so that nutritional objectives feature more prominently in those processes to result in proportionately greater allocations of public resources toward broad, effective programs and activities that assist the undernourished.

In none of the four case-study countries have the political leaders and policymakers effectively inserted nutrition considerations into the dominant policy discussions at the national level. They have also largely failed to reduce undernutrition. This failure is not because the problem of undernutrition is a politically contentious issue in any of the four countries. Rather, it is treated with considerable indifference in policy processes, the allocation of public resources, or the actions undertaken by the sectors and agencies of government. Nevertheless, the four countries provide some useful contrasts in the nature of their policy processes, administrative organizations, and their levels of economic and political development.

Although the geographical focus is Sub-Saharan Africa, many of the insights on policy processes and the problematic place of nutrition within such processes that can be drawn from this report are applicable in other parts of the developing world. However, the African focus does lead to some issues being considered that are irrelevant to other areas of the world that have different policy processes, levels and forms of economic development, nutritional challenges, or institutional frameworks.

The Agriculture–Nutrition Advantage Project Institutional Study

The case-study materials from Ghana, Mozambique, Nigeria, and Uganda used in this report originated in an institutional study of nutrition and agriculture that was undertaken by the Agriculture–Nutrition Advantage (TANA) project. This project, which ran from 2001 through 2004, aimed to strengthen and expand linkages between nutritionists and agriculturalists, particularly through employing gender-sensitive approaches, to reduce hunger and undernutrition in five countries in Africa—the four study countries and Kenya. The project was motivated by the sense that agriculture and nutrition communities were missing opportunities to reduce poverty, hunger, and malnutrition by failing to combine their efforts and scarce resources and to incorporate gender analysis into their work. If policymakers did take these steps as part of their regular operations, it would have an impact on poverty and malnutrition (ICRW/IFPRI 2004).

In each country, the project was centered on the activities of national project teams made up of agriculturalists, nutritionists, and gender specialists. The International Center for Research on Women and the International Food Policy Research Institute (IFPRI) implemented the project, using funding provided by the United States Agency for International Development (USAID).

The objective of the institutional study under the TANA project was to assess the extent to which the agriculture and nutrition communities in each country work as partners to reduce malnutrition, to gauge the potential gains from increased collaboration, and to understand the various constraints on such collaborations. The principal scale of analysis was at the national level. Two qualitative methods were used in the institutional study. First, key documents that focused on food and nutrition, agricultural sector development, and master development planning in each country were reviewed. The documentation obtained before fieldwork began served to guide the broad content of the interviews subsequently carried out in each country, the second method used. Between 30 and 40 semistructured interviews with agriculturalists, nutritionists, and policymakers were conducted in each country. Fieldwork for the institutional study was done in Uganda, Mozambique, and Nigeria between September and November 2002, while that for Ghana was done in March 2004. A final report on the study in the four countries was published later in 2004 (Benson et al. 2004).

This report draws on a subset of the information gathered in the institutional study done for the TANA project. A more narrow focus on nutrition in national policy processes is adopted here. The original study sought to develop a broad understanding in each country of the various government sectors and other actors involved in efforts to address undernutrition and how they work and interact. However, here I take a step back from that operational focus to consider more closely why mounting effective efforts in the public sector to address undernutrition is problematic in the first place. Consequently, much less attention is paid to the organization and priorities of the sectors whose actions might contribute to the aggregate nutritional status of the population. Rather, the aim here is to better understand the pattern of consistent underinvestment in efforts to reduce undernutrition in the four countries, regardless of the sectors concerned.

Organization of the Report

Drawing on the information gained through the institutional study, this report is organized in line with the twin objectives of (1) providing a general understanding on what makes it difficult for undernutrition to be targeted as a national development priority and (2) assessing several elements of the policy processes in the countries to guide efforts to place nutritional objectives more prominently in national policies. The next two chapters are primarily descriptive and conceptual in nature. Chapter 2 focuses on policy processes. Four elements of policy processes—structure, actors, narrative, and timing—and how policy changes emerge from their interplay are described in some detail to guide the empirical presentation of the results from each study country. A conceptual framework for the determinants of nutritional status is described in Chapter 3. The nature of these determinants is considered in light of what they imply for bringing about change in public policy to increase allocations of public resources that will improve the nutrition security of the undernourished.

The fourth chapter discusses the institutional study, providing additional detail on the TANA project, the methods employed in the study, and the study countries. Using the elements of the policy process described in Chapter 2 to organize the presentation, Chapter 5 reports on the findings of the institutional study country-by-country. This chapter ends with a cross-country assessment on the commonalities and important differences among the four countries. The final chapter draws on the information presented to suggest methods for increasing the allocations of public resources to assist the undernourished in the four countries.

CHAPTER 2

Policy Processes

Policies and how they are created are the focus of this chapter. The next chapter examines nutrition and nutrition policy by building on the broader understanding provided here. By policy, I mean authoritative decisions by which members of a community—whether national governments, local governments and communities, or the international community of nations—clarify their common interests and institute the means to attain and safeguard those interests (Clark 2002, 6). This definition of policy is relatively broad, covering both the process by which policies are created and the implementation of those policies. By definition, the policy process is political, so that the usually complex and unbalanced power relations among the participants, the degree to which participants need to be responsive to their various and often contentious constituencies, the management of multiple obligations, the different perspectives among the participants on the nature and salience of the policy problem, and the making of decisions under conditions of uncertainty, among other considerations, all interact to determine what policies will be in place at any given time (Porter 1994; Zahariadis 1999).

Before considering four key elements of the policy process—structures, actors, narrative, and timing—it is useful to recall why policies are important, at least in a normative sense. First, in line with the definition above, formal policies explicitly define what is considered to be the common good for the citizens of a nation or members of a community, at that point in time and given current political configurations. Policy serves as a statement of how government intends to prioritize its actions and expenditures. When citizens become sufficiently dissatisfied with the neglect of a particular problem by government, they can engage in the policy process to establish the priorities of government in addressing the problem. As such, particularly within representative, pluralistic governments, policy can serve as a check on personalized decisionmaking and abuse of power that works against the common good.

Second, statements of government policy enable citizens to hold government accountable. Policies define the duties of the government to its citizens. If policies are in place to foster social development, for example, the government is committing itself to allocate financial, human, and physical resources to that end. When these duties are not fulfilled and the actual allocation of resources by government is not in line with its stated priorities, affected citizens are justified in attempting to remedy the situation through the political process. Similarly, in many countries government agencies and other bodies making use of public resources must justify their use with reference to the policies guiding their allocation.

Finally, in the context of the developing countries of Sub-Saharan Africa, policy is an important map to guide how donors and other development partners allocate their support to that government. As such, policies are necessary for both bilateral and multilateral donors to prioritize the allocation of their aid to a country and to reassure their own constituents as to the appropriateness of how the funds were used.

Linear models of policymaking are frequently used to describe the discrete, logical steps of a decision process, from problem definition and agenda setting through decisionmaking to implementation, evaluation, and, finally, termination (deLeon 1999). In these models, problems motivate the development of policies, the identification of which typically is based on analysis of assembled evidence to drive technically optimal solutions, which are then implemented.

Although these linear models provide a useful description of the process for examining and understanding components of how choices are made to derive and implement policy, they hide the contentious and often recursive political character of the process (Jenkins-Smith and Sabatier 1993). Multiple and competing political interests at all stages in the process; different normative expectations, foundations of rationality, sources of knowledge, and consequently, perceptions of the policy problem and the validity of proposed solutions; varying degrees of attention to issues by political actors; and changes in the broader political context all serve to complicate linear models of policymaking. As Weiss (1977, 533) notes, "The policy making process is a political process, with the basic aim of reconciling interests in order to negotiate a consensus, not implementing logic and truth." Moreover, any consensus achieved reflects the relative power of the actors involved— characterizing any political processes as negotiations among equals will be much more the exception than the rule.

This report adopts this more challenging perspective on policymaking to better understand how nutrition and, specifically, combating undernutrition might receive more attention from a government. Four elements of the policy process are considered: the struc-

tures and institutions within which policies are established, the actors involved, the narratives used to define policy problems and solutions, and the circumstances under which policy decisions are made. Each of the first three elements—structures, actors, and narrative—interactively shapes the others (Keeley and Scoones 1999). The fourth element—the timing of policy changes— reflects the fact that policy change can result both from the dynamics of the other three elements and their interactions and from shifts in the broader conditions under which policymaking is undertaken.

Before considering each of these elements, three points should be highlighted. First, understanding particular policy processes requires understanding of the local situation. Policies are embedded within particular contexts: political, institutional, economic, and agroecological (Keeley and Scoones 1999). The context and the historical processes through which they emerged explain why one finds differing styles of policymaking in different places and times. Although this report seeks generalizations across the four study countries, I recognize that such generalizations will always be limited.

Second, much of the conceptual literature used here to understand policy processes and policy changes emerged from investigations of diffuse, adversarial policymaking processes that tend to be driven by organized interest groups in society, such as those found in many Western political systems (Neilson 2001). The interplay of such interest groups in the policy process, such as "advocacy coalitions" (Sabatier 1993) or "discourse coalitions" (Hajer 1995), is an important driver of policy change in these conceptual frameworks. As the nature of the policy processes in the study countries differs in several respects from such models, these concepts require adaptation for their use here. Notably, undernutrition as a problem in policy processes in the study countries has not resulted in the formation of engaged interests groups negotiating over conflicting perspectives on the issue.

Third, although the focus in this report is primarily on the definition of the policy problem, agenda setting, and decisionmaking within national policy processes, policymaking goes beyond decisionmaking to implementation. Policy implementation is as important as policy analysis and selection in attaining policy objectives. Following the identification of appropriate policy options, their subsequent implementation cannot be assumed. Funding constraints, political compromises, insufficiently trained workers, poor or perverse incentives, and local and bureaucratic political dynamics, among others, may all sabotage the implementation of policies that are technically optimal (Grindle and Thomas 1989). Bringing implementation into the subject matter expands the number of participants in the policy process and forces policy advocates to continue to engage in the process, even if they have secured government support for their policy initiative (Porter 1994). Moreover, it expands the scope of engagement for advocates in policy processes from the macrolevel of national policy formulation to the microscale of program implementation.

Policymaking Structures

The structures of policymaking referred to here reflect the institutional manifestations of the various components of the policy process. In this regard, the linear, rational model of policymaking is useful for identifying such structures, particularly in countries in the developed world with relatively complex political systems (Porter 1994). Thus, one can identify a set of policymaking structures associated with problem definition and agenda setting. In many countries these are formal political parties that may be formed on the basis of economic class, regional origin, or any of a range of other affiliation criteria and that engage in almost all aspects of political life. In addition, there

are special interest groups, such as industry lobby groups or voluntary, issue-focused groups emerging from civil society that are more selective in their engagements in the policy process. Within a democratic context at least, decisionmaking structures are primarily those that are instituted to enable decisions by citizen representatives—legislatures and cabinets. Finally, the policymaking structures associated with implementation are principally the government institutions that either regulate and provide oversight on key policies or, in the case of goods and services that typically are provided by the public sector, facilitate their provision.

In many developing countries, including the four countries examined in this study, democratic institutions at the national level are often absent or relatively new, so there is much less scope for a representative electoral system to influence problem definition and agenda setting for any policy debates. Similarly, civil society organizations, at least those that readily engage directly in policy processes, are quite weak. Often most of the relevant expertise on a particular policy issue is found within government, there being little effective demand in the nation for such specialized skills and knowledge outside of the public sector. This limitation is certainly the case with nutrition in the four study countries.

As a consequence, government institutions tend to play a significantly larger role in the earlier stages of policymaking—problem definition and policy decisionmaking—than is the case in those countries in which the linear, rational model of policy making is most often applied. Grindle and Thomas (1989, 244) usefully contrast the perspectives of society-centered explanations of policy choice with state-centered approaches. They argue that state-centered explanations that focus on the broad orientation of the state and the interactions of policy elites—"political and bureaucratic officials who have decision making responsibilities in government and whose decisions become authoritative for society"—provide a generally more useful starting point in examining policy decisionmaking in developing countries than do society-centered models that examine power relations, conflict, and negotiation among groups or classes in society. Although Grindle and Thomas (1989, 217) recognize that policy elites are "systematically constrained by societal interests, past policies, and historical and cultural legacies," even within these constraints, policy elites are able to exercise strategic leadership to bring about substantive changes in policy in most developing countries. My examination of nutrition policy in the four study countries similarly has found that a state-centered approach is useful. This approach is used in this report.

Although government agencies are the principal structures in the policy processes of the countries considered here, international donors and international nongovernmental organizations (NGOs) constitute important secondary elements. Given both the financial resources they bring and the expertise they can muster, these international development partners frequently motivate the setting of agendas on particular policy problems in such countries, remain active in support roles while decisions are made on policy, and frequently contribute significantly to the implementation of the policy, at least in the initial establishment of programs (Grindle 2004). Their participation is particularly salient in the social sectors, where new social initiatives are often funded almost exclusively from donor funding, at least in the study countries. Similarly, where there are insufficient numbers of trained personnel in government, international NGOs often are at the forefront in social service provision.

In highlighting government agencies and international development partners as significant structural components of the policy processes of developing countries, the intent is not to minimize the potential for

political parties or for special interest groups emerging from civil society to undertake important institutional functions in policy processes. However, such groups face daunting obstacles in building the necessary political capital and organization to engage effectively and sustainably in the policy process in a formal institutionalized manner. Policy elites who broker such processes are likely to safeguard their own interests by reducing the political resources of groups holding opposing views and limiting the latter's access to the venues in which the policy debates are conducted. Consequently, for those special interest groups that do participate in policy processes but whose perspectives differ from those managing the process, their continued participation in the processes should be expected to be increasingly under threat as the policy process advances (Sabatier and Jenkins-Smith 1999, 136). As such groups are relatively ineffectual in formal policy processes, they frequently will resort to the use of informal channels to further their interests (Grindle and Thomas 1991, 62–63). Whether such special interest groups feature as important structural elements in the policy processes of a country has to be established on a case-by-case basis. In the four countries considered in this study, their role generally has been quite limited in general and absent in nutrition-oriented policy processes.

Agents for Policy Change

A structural analysis of policy processes posits that negotiations for influence, protection of exclusive areas of competence, and competition for resources among sectors of the government bureaucracy account for any incremental dynamism in the policy processes in countries for which the state is the center of policy formulation (Keeley and Scoones 1999). Although varying with context, government institutions and the individuals in them also are held accountable by national leaders to safeguard the legitimacy of their regime. As such, there are political rewards for effective action, however defined. Consequently, there is sufficient impetus in these bureaucracies for policy processes to operate and change to occur. However, the policy changes that these government institutions undertake tend to be routine and incremental, rather than fundamental (Williamson 1999). The restructuring costs associated with fundamental change may well be seen as too great for any benefits obtained (Crewe and Young 2002).

However, the evidence does not support an assessment of policymaking and policy change exclusively focused on structural mechanisms in which individuals have no role. Policy change typically is motivated by agents. The "policy entrepreneur" is a figure seen in both state- and society-centered analyses of policy change. They are individuals or networks of concerned individuals who "influence policy through the ways in which they define problems, link them to solutions, . . . translate them into simplified images and understandings, . . . successfully mobilize the attention of policy makers, and sustain their interest in an issue or program over the longer run" (Porter 1994, 2). Indeed, in developing advocacy strategies to bring attention to problems requiring a policy response, a key strategy is to cultivate such an entrepreneur or champion to be the visible leader of the effort. Zahariadis (1999) argues that these individuals can be very effective, so long as they are well connected, persistent, and have access to many of the multiple arenas and institutional venues in which policy debates are undertaken, including the personal networks of government leaders, so that they can advance the policy choice they are championing. Within the context of nutrition, highly placed advocates who have access to political leaders have been key in several instances of significant changes in the priority given to public-sector efforts to combat undernutrition (Rokx 2000).

In the state-centered understanding of policymaking of Grindle and Thomas (1989), the agents of interest are the policy elite.

The authors demonstrate that these agents of change, although defined by their place in the state structures, nonetheless are capable of making space within those structures for significant policy changes. In doing so, a combination of individual self-interest, a broader vision of the public interest, considerations of social pressures and threats to the legitimacy of the state, and their own "experience, study, values, ideology, institutional affiliation, and professional training" serve to motivate them in seeking policy change (Grindle and Thomas 1991, 19). Although enmeshed in the policymaking and administrative structures of the state, they are able to make choices as individuals and to act on them.

In society-centered analyses of policy change, considerably more room for action is given to individuals and coalitions. Those at the center of the advocacy coalition framework of the policy process are "actors from a variety of public and private institutions at all levels of government who share a set of basic beliefs (basic values, causal assumptions, and problem perceptions) and who seek to manipulate the rules, budgets, and personnel of governmental institutions in order to achieve these goals over time" (Jenkins-Smith and Sabatier 1993, 5). It is the individual convictions of the participants in these advocacy coalitions—their own belief systems—that provide the impetus and direction to their efforts to bring about policy change.

Conceptually, this focus on the actors involved in the policy process breaks down some of the boundaries that are defined when examining the structural elements of the process. Advocacy networks that develop around an issue can have a membership extending across boundaries of institutions that a structural analysis would see as likely being in opposition on policy issues. As discussed in more detail in the next chapter, effective action to address undernutrition requires action by several sectors of government, each of which has separate objectives and skills—health, education, water and sanitation, and agriculture. Of course, to foster an advocacy network or coalition with such a disparate membership requires the trade-off of a necessarily loose organizational form (Sabatier and Jenkins-Smith 1999). However, this loose form does not preclude such coalitions from being active or effective in the policy process.

In most of the literature on policy change, whether state- or society-centered, the key actors considered come from a relatively specialized subset of the population that consists of generally high-level individuals from the public and private sectors and civil society who are actively concerned with a policy problem and its implementation. This situation stands in contrast to many exhortations to use participatory processes to bring about sustainable, deep-seated policy change in many developing countries (for example, see UNDP 1993; World Bank 2003). Are there significant strategic advantages in developing broad-based participatory involvement in a coalition advocating for policy change? From an instrumental vantage point on short- to medium-term policy change, Sabatier argues a realist view that "significant changes in the influence of various social groups normally takes several decades" (1993, 21). Consequently, developing a broad-based participatory approach and seeking to bring into an advocacy coalition large disadvantaged and currently politically inert groups within society—"latent constituencies"— likely is not justified, because a coalition seeking policy change determines how to allocate its scarce political resources in the medium term. The benefits that would accrue to the policy change effort of the coalition from such an initiative are likely to be slim. Keeley and Scoones (1999, 33) disagree, however, contending that "public perceptions and values matter, and inclusionary reflection may be essential to the development of social trust" and that "there is always the possibility for new and unpredicted development of policy to take place as a consequence of the agency and inter-action of different actors." However, in calling for such broad participation in establishing policy, Keeley and Scoones acknowledge that there are immense challenges involved in developing inclusive policy processes. In sum, although there may be important normative reasons for a broadly participatory approach in seeking policy change, in the actual engagement with policy processes, the short-term practical advantages of doing so are less clear.

Policy Narrative

For a problem to become a policy issue, it needs to be recognized as a problem that is solvable in part through government efforts. The definition and framing of a problem is itself a key element in the policy process. As Hajer (1995, 15) notes, "policy making can be analyzed as a set of practices that are meant to process fragmented and contradictory statements to be able to create the sort of problems that institutions can handle and for which solutions can be found. Hence, policies are not only devised to solve problems, problems also have to be devised to be able to create policies." Whether an issue is seen as a problem requiring a public response is dependent on how the issue is defined and how a storyline is constructed for conveying an accepted understanding of the significance and causes of the problem and what action is required to tackle it. Such policy narratives define the world and provide an interpretation of cause and effect relationships in a way that, if successful, is recognized as valid by others engaged in the policy process and excludes from consideration alternative definitions and interpretations. As more and more participants in the policy process subscribe to the interpretation provided by the narrative, support builds for the policy prescriptions it provides.

These narratives can have an influence in the policy process that is independent of those initially responsible for constructing the narrative (Stone 2001). In the realm of international development, for example, one can point to a broad range of such narratives that seek to motivate policy change —narratives on the centrality to development of economic growth, poverty reduction, meeting basic needs (for example, the United Nations Millennium Development Goals), improving governance, and so on. "In a world of complexity, where multiple issues compete for attention, this ability to distil a clear, simple, and pressing narrative should not be underestimated" (Keeley and Scoones 2003, 53).

Policy research contributes to the construction of a policy narrative. Policy narratives generally find part of their justification in technical information that stands up to close scrutiny. However, "technical data seldom speak for themselves. If usable knowledge is the objective, then an active process of claim making and persuasion needs to follow the production of scientifically defensible argumentation" (Porter 1994, 2). For any participant in an effort to bring about policy change, this process requires consideration of how the facts might best be selected, interpreted, and presented in light of the characteristics of the policy process at hand and desired policy outcomes, so that other participants respond positively.

An important concept in understanding policy processes is related to the nature of the policy problem. Its nature is defined through dominant policy narratives. Grindle and Thomas (1989, 232) usefully distinguish "pressing" and "chosen" policy problems. They note that when the policy concern is pressing, substantive policy reform is more likely to occur than when the concern is treated as politics-as-usual and policymakers can choose not to address the issue without risking their positions of leadership.

Of course, this perception of crisis is itself an element of how a policy problem is framed. Grindle and Thomas (1989, 228) argue that crises are those situations when the political or economic health or survival of the regime is at stake. However, alternative narratives on particular policy problems can lead to different perceptions of the problem's urgency. Moreover, a multiple layering and interaction of narratives can result in diverse assessments in different contexts of the conditions under which a government can be judged to be in crisis. With creative advocacy on a politics-as-usual issue, policy narratives might be crafted that could call into question the legitimacy of a regime based on its attention to the issue. There is nothing inherent to a policy problem that necessarily leads one to characterize it as either pressing or chosen. The framing and definition of the policy issue is critical to the characterization it receives.

Finally, an important consideration in developing a storyline as part of an effort to foster policy change is that it should reflect and be supportive of the master development policy framework of government, making clear exactly how the policy problem is inhibiting the attainment of the overall goals of government and how the solutions advocated will propel society toward those goals. Governments should seek broad consistency in their policies, so that their agencies do not work at cross purposes. Moreover, "earlier decisions form a matrix of policy into which new decisions must fit" (Horowitz 1989, 203). Consequently, one should expect both path dependency and some hierarchy within the overall policy processes of a government: earlier policy decisions constrain how those that follow are framed, and subordinate, sectoral policies should be consistent and supportive of overarching policies and priorities.

Timing of Policy Change

The interaction of the institutions involved in policy process, the efforts of the actors, and the manner in which the policy problem and solutions are presented will not necessarily result in any change in policy. The success of the efforts of actors in the policy process to bring about change in the priorities of government and in the allocation of its resources is not solely determined by the quality and persistence of their own efforts.

Policy change is contingent on circumstances. Across the literature on policy change, there is recognition of the importance of fortuitous timing in bringing about such change.

Kingdon's (1995) policy-streams model of policy change provides a useful understanding of the role of timing. He posits three streams of activity by which actors can affect policy processes: (1) defining a problem as being of public concern, (2) formulating policy solutions, and (3) obtaining political consensus. However, these streams are not sequential, but operate simultaneously and independently of one another. Windows of opportunity to instigate policy change occur infrequently when the three streams converge—that is, when an important policy problem is broadly recognized and a clear policy solution is available at the same time as significant and wide political interest in the issue emerges. As Porter (1994, 11) notes, effective advocacy networks and their leaders "push their proposals all the time, whether a window is open or not. They try to make linkages among problems, solutions, and politics long before a window opens so they are ready with a prepackaged policy initiative when it does."

Although giving less credit to the agency of the advocates involved, Sabatier and Jenkins-Smith (1999, 147) similarly suggest that major change in a policy subsystem is only possible when there are significant events or shocks in the broader system. In particular, they identify changes in government, public opinion, general socio-economic conditions, or in other policy sectors as necessary for any substantial change to occur in a policy subsystem. While not characterizing the competitive activities of advocacy coalitions within a policy subsystem as misguided or wasted, Sabatier (1993, 29) asserts that "major shifts in the distribution of political resources will usually be the product of events external to the subsystem and largely external to activities of subsystem coalitions." As Horowitz (1989, 205) observed, "a disproportionate number of policies are adopted at exceptional times . . . when the system is not functioning as it usually does." In explaining policy change, circumstance is a key element.

In this chapter, a conceptual approach was taken to examine key elements of how policies are created and changed, particularly in central governments, without paying much attention to the actual content of the policies. Four important elements of policymaking were discussed—policymaking structures, the agents who work to bring about policy change, the narratives that are used, and the timing of changes. In the chapters that follow, I focus on the issue of nutrition in policymaking, using the four elements described in this chapter to assess how undernutrition as a policy problem has been addressed and what opportunities might be exploited to gain increased national government support for efforts to reduce the prevalence of undernutrition in Ghana, Mozambique, Nigeria, and Uganda.

CHAPTER 3

Nutrition as a Public Policy Concern

In line with the idea presented in the previous chapter that an important element in policy-making is how the policy problem is framed, the problem of undernutrition is described in more detail in this chapter. I use the concept of nutrition security as the objective of efforts to reduce undernutrition, so I first briefly define the concept and several related terms. Then a conceptual framework of the determinants of nutritional status is presented, followed by a brief demographic description of the nutritionally vulnerable in society toward whom public efforts should be targeted. Turning to policy in reducing undernutrition, I discuss the principal justifications used to argue that undernutrition must be treated as a public policy problem. The conceptual framework then is used to provide an understanding of why developing effective policy to address undernutrition is often problematic and, when such policy is formulated, is often difficult to implement successfully.

A Conceptual Framework of the Determinants of Nutritional Status

Defining Nutrition Security

A household achieves nutrition security when it has secure access to food coupled with a sanitary environment, adequate health services, and knowledgeable care to ensure a healthy life for all household members. Nutrition security is as concerned with the utilization of the food obtained by a household as with access to this food, but the concept goes beyond food alone. An individual's nutritional status is related directly to both diet and health. The nature of these two components, in turn, is determined by the food security status of the household in which the individual resides, and, critically, by the availability of health services, a healthy environment, and the quality of care the individual receives.

Although the focus of this report is on undernutrition and how policy might be formulated and implemented to assist the nutritionally insecure, these terms are quite broad and are often used in an imprecise manner. Figure 3.1 and Box 3.1 define these and related terms. In Figure 3.1, the outer oval represents a nutritionally insecure population. The various shapes within the oval and their overlaps represent members of that population—whether households or individuals—who are suffering from various forms of nutrition insecurity, particularly as related to food insecurity.[1] Additional distinctions in these terms are provided in the definitions in Box 3.1.

---

[1]The overlap of the "Overnourished" oval with the "Food insecure" oval reflects emerging evidence that obesity is in some cases a result of moderately food-insecure households relying on cheaper, high-fat, high-caloric, and less nutritious foods, because they are unable to afford a balanced, but more costly, diet (Townsend et al. 2001).

Figure 3.1 Overlapping concepts in the context of nutrition insecurity

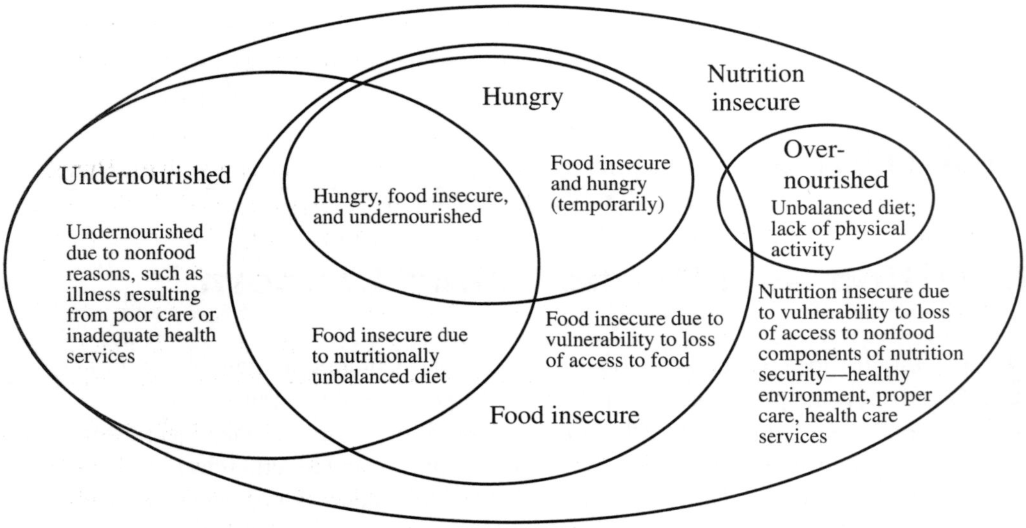

Source: Adapted from HTF (2003).

Determinants of Nutritional Status—A Conceptual Framework

The global conceptual framework of the determinants of nutritional status presents a generalized understanding of how undernutrition is the outcome of a multisectoral development problem that can be analyzed in terms of immediate, underlying, and basic determinants (Figure 3.2). This framework has become one of the most familiar concepts in international public nutrition over the past decade, fostering improved understanding and dialogue about the nature and causes of malnutrition and the actions needed to address problems of malnutrition.

Although nutritional status is an individual-level characteristic, the determinants of nutritional status extend beyond the control of the household of which an individual is a member into the realm of policy and government that is the focus of this report. Examining the conceptual framework from the perspective of undernutrition, its immediate

determinants are the mutually reinforcing conditions of inadequate dietary intake and infectious disease. Its underlying determinants are household food insecurity, inadequate maternal and child care, inadequate health services, and an unhealthy environment. Finally, its basic determinants include formal and nonformal institutions; political, economic, and ideological structures and systems; and their dynamics. These basic determinants govern the degree to which society operates effectively to safeguard the nutrition security of its vulnerable members.

The degree to which the three underlying determinants of nutritional status are expressed positively or negatively is a question of available resources. These include the availability of food, the physical and economic access that an individual or household has to that food, the caregiver's[2] knowledge of how to utilize available food and to properly care for the individual, the caregiver's own health status, and the con-

---

[2]"Caregiver" refers to the household member primarily responsible for food preparation and caring for young children and the infirm.

Box 3.1   Definitions of Terms Related to Nutrition Security

Nutritional status: The physiological condition of an individual that results from the balance between nutrient requirements and intake and the ability of the body to use these nutrients.

Hunger: People experience the sensation of hunger when they lack the basic food intake necessary to provide them with the energy and nutrients for active lives. Hunger principally refers to inadequate consumption of the macronutrients, carbohydrates in particular, and, when involuntary, is an outcome of food insecurity. All involuntarily hungry people are food insecure, but not all food-insecure people are hungry.

Malnutrition: A physical condition or process that results from the interaction of improper diet and illness. It is commonly reflected in excess morbidity and mortality in adults and children alike. Undernutrition and overnutrition are two forms of malnutrition.

Undernutrition: Malnutrition caused by inadequate food intake or poor absorption or biological use of nutrients consumed because of illness, disease, or nutrient imbalance. In addition to an absolute deficit in food intake, undernutrition can result from imbalanced diets in which sufficient macronutrients are consumed (carbohydrates, fat, protein) but insufficient vitamins and minerals (in particular, the micronutrients iron, iodine, zinc, and vitamin A), resulting in various physiological disorders and increased susceptibility to disease.

   Although most individuals suffering from undernutrition are food insecure, an individual or household can be food secure but undernourished. For example, an individual who is food secure but suffers from frequent and severe bouts of diarrhea is not able to use the food for growth and development and is experiencing undernutrition.

Overnutrition: Malnutrition caused by an excess of certain nutrients (such as saturated fats and added sugars) in combination with low levels of physical activity that may result in obesity, heart disease and other circulatory disorders, diabetes, and similar diseases. Although most individuals suffering from overnutrition are food secure, they do not enjoy nutrition security. Most malnourished individuals in developing countries are undernourished, but problems of overnutrition are also present and increasing.

Vulnerability: The presence of factors that place people at risk of becoming food insecure or malnourished, whether from loss of access to food, proper nutritional care, or an inability to physiologically utilize available food because of infection or other disease.

Sources: FIVIMS/FAO (2002); HTF (2003).

---

trol the caregiver has over resources in the household that might be used to nourish the individual. Additionally, a broad range of goods and services whose provision often involves public agencies contributes to determining the nutritional status of an individual. These include the level of access to information and services for maintaining health, whether curative services are available, and the presence or absence of a healthy environment with clean water, adequate sanitation, and proper shelter. To define priorities for action to assist the undernourished in meeting their nutritional needs, the relative importance of each determinant must be assessed and analyzed in context. A

Figure 3.2   Conceptual framework of the determinants of nutritional status

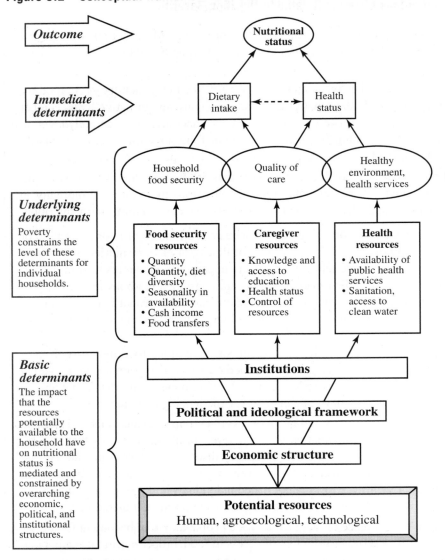

Sources: Adapted from UNICEF (1990), Jonsson (1993), and Smith and Haddad (2000).

sustained healthy and active life is only possible when these underlying determinants are present and are of appropriate quality.

Two important points arise from the nature of the underlying determinants of nutritional status. First, the three underlying determinants make explicit that multiple sectors need to be involved in any comprehensive effort to improve the general nutritional status of the population. For example, agriculture is important for the quantity and

quality of food available; education, so that the nutritional care provided is appropriate; health care, so people can effectively utilize available nutrients; and so on across most sectors. Any one sector operating alone without parallel efforts by other sectors likely will not succeed in significantly enhancing nutrition security in a sustainable manner. Expertise to address the problem is not only located within the health sector. Undernutrition is not simply a medical problem that is solely addressed in a technical and scientific manner, but a social policy problem of concern to multiple sectors.

Second, the overlapping ovals of food, health, and care in Figure 3.2 imply that these three underlying determinants are related to one another in complex ways. These interrelationships must be analyzed and properly understood in a given context to design appropriate remedies. For instance, foodsecure households may still have undernourished children and women, because the burden of women's agricultural and other work or inadequate knowledge may compromise the quality of child care, or culturally defined practices of food preparation or consumption may result in deficient or improper diets for young children or their mothers. Moreover, efforts to increase household food security may either increase or decrease levels of undernutrition in the household, depending upon how these increases in production are achieved. Similar contingencies exist between care and health.

The quality of the underlying determinants of nutritional status for a household is dependent to a considerable degree on the distribution of available resources in society. That is, the availability of nutritional resources at the household level is linked to a set of basic determinants that are a function of how society is organized in terms of economic structure, political and ideological expectations, and the institutions through which social interactions are regulated, social values are met, and potential resources are converted into actual resources. Policy processes constitute a central means by which decisions are made as to what should be the broad objectives and priorities of a society and how its resources should be allocated to those ends. As such, they are one of the basic determinants of nutritional status shown at the bottom of Figure 3.2. Consequently, this conceptual framework is a useful basis for examining how nutrition concerns can be addressed more effectively in policy processes.

Nutritionally Vulnerable Target Groups

The individuals whose nutritional status is of most concern are children younger than 2 years and pregnant and lactating women. In formulating priorities for addressing undernutrition, these two nutritionally vulnerable demographic groups should be targeted. This focus reflects a coincidence of both biological and economic considerations. In most low-income countries, faltering growth begins in the first 6 months of life—age-specific prevalence rates for undernutrition generally increase with age until about 2 years of age and then level off (Shrimpton et al. 2001). Rarely does a child who is stunted at age 2 fully recover his or her growth deficit in later years—to a large degree, the stunting is permanent. Thus, the window of opportunity to prevent undernutrition is relatively narrow. This vulnerable age bracket is also the time of peak child mortality, as well as the time that a child's brain is growing most rapidly. Preventing undernutrition at this age can avoid comparatively ineffective later attempts to reverse the health and cognitive impairments resulting from undernutrition (World Bank 2006a, 12).

Pregnancy is also a period of relatively high risk and, correspondingly, a time that preventative measures can be most effective. Folate or iodine deficiency in early pregnancy can cause irreversible defects in the child. Similarly, iron deficiency anemia increases the risk of maternal mortality and of low birthweight babies. High-energy outlay or low food intake by the mother in her third trimester of pregnancy can also lead to low birthweight. Undernourished mothers give birth to undernourished babies.

Thus, not only does failure to address the nutritional needs of pregnant women and very young children generally lead to lasting consequences for the child, as shown in Figure 3.3, these consequences transmit over generations through a cycle of undernutrition, ill health, poverty, and diminished

Figure 3.3   The transmission of undernutrition and its consequences across generations

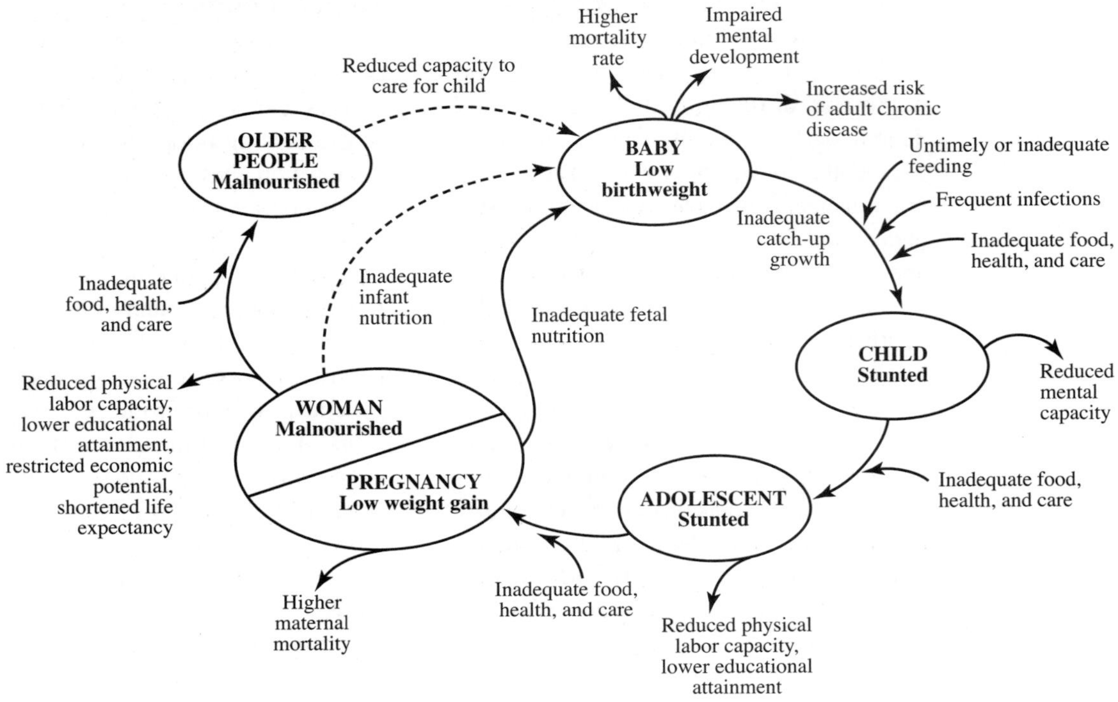

Source: Adapted from ACC/SCN-IFPRI (2000).

human and economic potential. Individuals who were undernourished as children will earn less on average than their well-nourished neighbors and, therefore, have fewer resources to provide their own children. Women who were malnourished as children have a higher risk of adverse pregnancy outcomes when they become mothers (Ramakrishnan et al. 1999) and are more likely to give birth to infants with low birthweight, who will face the effects of malnutrition diminishing their physical and intellectual potential from the day they are born.

Addressing Undernutrition through Public Policy

Now I consider the justifications for treating undernutrition as an issue of public concern in developing countries in Sub-Saharan Africa and, building on the discussion of policy processes in the previous chapter, why effective policy to address undernutrition might be problematic to develop and implement.

Why Undernutrition Requires a Public-Policy Response

To release the economic and human potential of a well-nourished population, nutrition advocates assert that the state must provide key goods and services that will enable individuals to meet their nutritional needs. General improved nutrition will not result simply from economic development: specific actions to address undernutrition are needed.

However, before considering the role that nutrition plays in economic and human development, it should be recognized that there is merit in reducing undernutrition and the associated suffering it causes simply because it is the right thing to do. Broadly accepted normative justifications exist for addressing undernutrition. Adequate nutrition has long been recognized as a fundamental human right, enshrined in key international conventions. Freedom from hunger and malnutrition was declared a basic human right in the 1948 Universal Declaration of Human Rights (United Nations General Assembly 1948), which is widely accepted as the basic charter of internationally recognized human rights. The convention asserts that "everyone has the right to a standard of living adequate for the health and well-being of himself and his family" (Article 25). Article 11 of the International Covenant of Economic, Social, and Cultural Rights (United Nations General Assembly 1966, Article 11, 1) reaffirms this by "recognizing the fundamental right of everyone to be free from hunger," with the signatory states, or parties to the covenant, committing to take the measures to realize this right, including "disseminating knowledge of the principles of nutrition" (Article 11, 2a). As children are among the most vulnerable to malnutrition and most likely to suffer its consequences over the long term, this principle also was reinforced in the 1989 Convention on the Rights of the Child (United Nations General Assembly 1989), which has been ratified by most national governments. Article 24 of the Convention states that "States Parties recognize the right of the child to enjoyment of the highest attainable standard of health" and shall act appropriately "to combat disease and malnutrition" through the provision of "adequate nutritious foods, clean drinking-water, and healthcare." The right to nutrition security also is upheld in many national constitutions, committing the government to ensure that these nutritional rights are respected, especially among the most vulnerable.

However, beyond ensuring that the citizens of a country are properly nourished simply as a duty of the state, important economic reasons provide justification for the engagement of the state on this issue. There are important positive externalities for society as a whole to any investments that reduce undernutrition—indeed, the basic economic justification for the public sector to improve nutrition is to ensure that its socie-tal benefits are realized beyond what private investments might provide. The adverse physical, cognitive, and economic consequences of undernutrition for the individual play out throughout his or her life and, when aggregated across all of the undernourished, result in substantial economic costs for a country's economy:

• Undernutrition in young children leads to higher mortality and the loss of the economic potential of these individuals.
• Survivors of severe undernutrition have higher morbidity, requiring additional health care services and diversion of the time and labor of their caregivers within the household from other productive activities.
• Undernutrition leads to lower cognitive development, lower IQs, and thus, slower learning throughout life, even after the child is no longer undernourished. For example, it was found that individuals who were malnourished as preschoolers in rural Zimbabwe completed on average 0.7 fewer years of schooling than would have been the case if they had been adequately nourished (Alderman, Hoddinott, and Kinsey 2003).
• Once in the workforce, additional productivity losses associated with workers who were previously undernourished arise from the direct links between stunted physical stature and reduced physical productivity and between decreased cognitive abilities and impaired faculties for performing specialized technical tasks. The same rural Zimbabwe study found that childhood undernutrition contributed to a loss of lifetime earnings of 7–12 percent relative to the earnings of those who were properly nourished (Alderman, Hoddinott, and Kinsey 2003).

With their comparatively high rates of undernutrition, the countries of Sub-Saharan Africa each lose hundreds of millions of dollars of productivity every year to these types of nutrition-related impairments. For example, the annual economic costs to Ethiopia of child stunting and iodine deficiencies alone have been estimated at more than $450 million, or 0.70 percent of the annual national gross domestic product (GDP; Ethiopian PROFILES Team and AED/Linkages 2005).

Given these consequences of malnutrition, programs that prevent malnutrition have been shown to have high economic rates of returns. Behrman, Alderman, and Hoddinott (2004) demonstrated that every dollar spent on including nutrition in integrated programs promoting child health will lead to a return of 10 dollars in increased earnings and lower medical costs, even when future earnings are discounted using standard accounting procedures. Promotion of proper breastfeeding has similar high rates of return. Returns to micronutrient interventions through fortification and supplementation generally are even higher, reflecting the comparatively low cost of providing the supplements.

Although the public costs of undernutrition are very large and the returns to public investments in reducing undernutrition are considerable, this fact alone does not necessarily mean that public resources should be allocated directly to reducing undernutrition. Increases in income plausibly could enable households to privately invest in their own nutritional well-being and thereby take the problem of undernutrition out of the public domain. Could robust economic growth on its own significantly reduce malnutrition?

In considering this question, it is clear that economic growth does lead to reduced malnutrition. This reduction has been demonstrated in cross-country studies as well as comparisons of nutritional status among different income groups within countries. A cross-country study estimated that child underweight (low weight for age) rates globally would decline by 27 percent by 2015 from their levels in the 1990s

if countries maintain per capita income growth of 2.5 percent per year (Haddad et al. 2003). However, few countries have been able to sustain such a rate of economic growth: Between 1980 and 2004, only six countries in Sub-Saharan Africa registered annual GDP per capita growth rates above 2.5 percent for 13 or more of the 25 years of this period (World Bank 2006b). Moreover, there is considerable variation in the effects of economic growth on undernutrition across countries. For example, Christiaensen and Alderman (2004) estimated that 2.5 percent per capita income growth in Ethiopia for 15 years would only reduce undernutrition by between 3 and 4 percent. Although higher rates of income growth will make greater inroads, in the absence of specific programs targeted at reducing and preventing undernutrition, levels of undernutrition tend to decline at half the rate that per capita income grows (Haddad et al. 2003, 121).

Furthermore, several of the key determinants of undernutrition are linked to deficiencies in key goods and services whose provision typically is the responsibility of the public sector—inadequate health services, poor water and sanitation services, limited or inappropriate training on proper nutritional care, and the like. In the short term, increases in private household incomes are unlikely to alter the quality of the provision of these goods and services or their quantity. There is likely to be a considerable lag between sustained income growth, the provision of these goods and services, and corresponding reductions in the aggregate undernutrition levels in a country.

Thus, even under conditions of general economic growth, without dedicated programs to ensure that these key nutrition-related services are provided, many children will face undernourishment, with all of the human and economic costs such a condition brings (Haddad et al. 2003). These programs include vitamin A supplementation, salt iodization, iron supplementation for pregnant women, and regular monitoring of child growth with follow-up action, as well as broader investments in health and sanitation, in specific programs to convey knowledge about child care, and in measures to improve food security (World Bank 2006a).

The evidence is strong that timely and high economic returns result from dedicated programs to reduce undernutrition—the immense burden of the economic costs associated with undernutrition is reduced, while sustained nutrition security results in economically more productive and creative citizens. Thus, the arrow of causation between better nutritional status and economic growth can be interpreted to run in both directions (Mason 2000). Indeed, there is compelling evidence that the arrow of causation is stronger from improved nutritional status and similar investments in human development to economic growth than the reverse. At the national level, Ranis, Stewart, and Ramirez (2000) show that countries that prioritize investments in human development (education, health, nutrition, and the like) over those focused directly on economic growth are more likely to achieve both objectives than those that prioritize direct actions to achieve economic growth. Human development is an important element of the enabling environment for economic growth. In any case, applying this analysis to the household level, undernutrition is both an outcome of and an important contributor to poverty. Building the capacity of households to attain nutrition security is an element of broad economic growth and poverty reduction.

What Is a Nutrition Policy?

The focus of this research report is on addressing nutrition in national policy processes. Consequently, in the discussion that follows, considerable attention is paid to the national nutrition policies of the study countries. However, it is reasonable to ask how one would recognize such a policy. A nutrition policy establishes generally improved nutrition as an objective of the state toward which it allocates resources. Such a policy outlines the processes and activities that the government will undertake or support to improve nutrition in the country substantially. Moreover, it should provide some guidance on establishing an institutional framework for implementation and on identifying who is responsible for ensuring that the specific activities called for in the policy are successfully carried out.

In many cases, including in three of the four countries examined here, formal nutrition policy statements have been developed. However, such documents are not required, nor are they necessarily effective in ensuring that improved nutrition is given priority. In the end, government policy on nutrition is best revealed by reviewing the choices that a government makes with respect to how it allocates its human, financial, and physical resources to efforts to improve nutrition or supports similar efforts by its development partners. Where it can be observed that improved nutritional outcomes are important criteria for monitoring the performance of government agencies and appropriate allocations of public resources have been made, the basic elements of an effective nutrition policy are in place, even if such a policy has not been developed formally.

Within the broader policy context of a government, any nutrition policy, whether formal or informal, must be consistent with the government's master development strategy. However, for nutrition objectives to be given due consideration across the government, it is important that those objectives be clearly stated in that master development strategy. Similarly, given the problematic fit of nutrition within the sectoral organization of the government bureaucracy (because of the multisectoral nature of the determinants of improved nutrition), the elements of a nutrition policy need also to be coherent with the policies of the sectors whose actions might contribute to improved nutrition. However, a nutrition policy will not necessarily be dependent on the priorities established by each sector. The nutrition policy can be used to ensure that sectoral policy decision-makers take into account the important contributions that their sector can make to attaining sustained significant improvements in nutritional status in the population.

Finally, a common element in most formal nutrition policy statements is the establishment of an institution that coordinates nutrition policy across multiple sectors. Such institutional bodies are seen in the three countries with formal nutrition policies examined here. This coordination function is not an inherent element of state action to contribute to improved nutrition, however. If the various sectors whose actions contribute to improved nutrition were provided with sufficient resources and leadership to carry out their mandates, improved nutrition would be among the complementary benefits that would result. However, where resources are limited and not all sectoral priorities can be attained, coordination is often needed to ensure that complementary activities are undertaken jointly (or in proper sequence) by the sectors concerned. Coordination, with appropriate authority, often is needed to ensure that all of the various sectoral elements necessary for improved nutrition are in place.

Challenges Facing Action on Nutrition in National Policy Processes

For normative, instrumental, and pragmatic reasons, a strong case can be made for the importance of addressing the needs of the undernourished as an issue of public concern and, hence, the desirability of governments to prioritize and make substantial investments in efforts to reduce undernutrition among their citizens. However, persistantly high levels of undernutrition in many developing countries, particularly in Sub-Saharan Africa, show that nutrition is effectively absent from the list of priorities of most of these countries. Building on the insights provided by the conceptual framework of the determinants of nutritional status, here I examine several reasons that explain why there may be a lack of broad action on the

part of governments to address undernutrition. These explanations will be examined empirically when I turn to the country case studies later in this report.

Poor Understanding of the Prevalence and Causes of Undernutrition. Undernutrition is often hidden. It requires knowledge to identify the threat to well-being that undernutrition presents, to understand its causes in a particular context, and to take action against it, whether one is a parent with an undernourished child or a policymaker judging how best to allocate state resources. Heaver (2002, 24) notes that politicians and development planners often underinvest in nutrition simply because they do not see the damage that undernutrition is doing to the health, intellectual capacity, and productivity of the people or understand how to address the problem. This characteristic of undernutrition can pose a major obstacle both to building demand for action against it and for instituting proper action.

Similarly, the lack of a holistic appreciation of its causes may result in an abundance of experts on the sectoral subcomponents of what is needed to improve nutrition —agricultural experts, health care personnel, sanitation experts, teachers, and so on. However, usually there are far fewer nutritionists available who can use the conceptual framework of the determinants of nutritional status in an inclusive manner to ensure that nutrition-related activities are properly coordinated or sequenced across the various sectors. Human capacity in both public and clinical nutrition is necessary to gauge the severity and causes of undernutrition in the population and guide the broad range of actions needed to address the problem.

Low Political Demand for Action against Undernutrition. The undernourished are politically weak. Poor nutritional status is among the outcomes of a lack of political voice and participation in public debate guiding the development process (Sen 1999). The nutritionally vulnerable are among those groups with the weakest direct representation in political arenas virtually throughout the world, whose demands are likely to go unheard. Moreover, they often lack knowledge on the causes of under-nutrition that is necessary to articulate clear political demands. Given that those who would directly and immediately benefit from nutrition interventions are a weak and silent political constituency, political leaders can ignore them and their nutritional concerns with few political consequences. Consequently, particularly when coupled with the knowledge gap that must be bridged concerning malnutrition, "there is minimal 'effective demand' for nutrition at the community level, and frequently at governmental levels as well" (Levinson 2000, 2).

Multisectoral Nature of Nutrition. That part of the conceptual framework detailing the underlying determinants of nutritional status emphasizes the multisectoral nature of any comprehensive effort to improve the general nutritional status of the population. This multisectoral nature of nutrition poses two challenges. First, no one formal sector of government can be expected to take primary responsibility for improving nutrition in the population. All of the sectors that have responsibility for some elements of the determinants of nutritional status may be intellectually committed to the goal of improved nutrition. However, pragmatically, improved nutrition will not be used as a performance indicator for any of the sectors. They all have their particular sectoral mandates, into which nutrition does not fit neatly and wholly. Consequently, each sector can give nutrition concerns secondary priority and, when necessary, safely ignore it and still satisfactorily meet its primary mandate.

Second, individual leadership is more critical if cross-cutting issues, such as nutrition, are to be prioritized. An important consequence of the poor sectoral fit of nutrition is that the institutional organization of the sectors does not produce any natural institutional champions or advocates for nutrition at the highest levels of government. Within the policy process, no leaders of formal government institutions necessarily see themselves as responsible for ensuring that sufficient state resources are allocated to addressing undernutrition and that the multiple determinants of the problem are addressed. Without such leadership and given limited resources and human capacity, the routine operations of government through the various agencies are unlikely to lead to effective public efforts to address undernutrition. Because politicians and other members of the policy elite are unlikely to automatically increase the resources allocated to activities that enhance nutrition security, the motivation to do so must come from elsewhere. Advocacy efforts are more central to bringing attention and commitment to cross-sectoral problems, such as undernutrition, than for those that neatly fit within the sectoral organization of government.

In the face of this awkward place of nutrition, governments have sought to establish an official place for nutrition in the institutional framework of government and, hence, national policy processes. As will be described in more detail in the country case studies in Chapter 5, such bodies have been incorporated into the institutional framework of the national governments in Mozambique, Nigeria, and Uganda. However, the track records of such multisectoral nutrition councils in shifting government resource allocations to address undernutrition are quite poor. There are several reasons why these institutions tend to be ineffective. Perhaps most salient is that sectoral ministries tend to view themselves as being in competition with one another for resources. Most participants in the budgeting process assume that resources allocated to another sector are lost to their own. The opinion offered by the nutrition officer from one of the states of Nigeria was shared quite widely by respondents across the study countries: "Funding is at the core of why there is little interaction between agriculture and health. Everyone wants to be in charge. If [the Ministry of] Health writes nutrition proposals that include some agricultural components, Agriculture is unhappy with Health, as Agriculture feels that Health is trying to take resources that should be theirs." A cross-sectoral body, such as a food security and nutrition council, does not fit this sectoral pattern of resource allocation and adds a layer of complexity to it.

Developing a home for nutrition issues in the policy and administrative institutions of government does not ensure that increased resources are allocated to addressing undernutrition. Indeed, the fact that virtually all programmatic costs for nutrition programs in the four study countries are borne by donors and not by government indicates that such multisectoral nutrition councils lack influence in this regard. However, the creation of such institutions does have some value. First, where working relationships among institutions carrying out nutrition activities are largely maintained through the personal ties among a small group of nutritionists, these relationships are at risk when there is turnover in personnel. Longer term efforts to address undernutrition are more likely to be successful with an institutionalized nutrition coordination council in place. Second and more important for my objectives here, the process of analysis, negotiation, and priority setting through which these councils are established is valuable in itself to develop strategies to address undernutrition in the national context. Moreover, the resultant legitimacy that such councils are accorded in the policy processes of government provides an entry for nutrition advocates into policy debates. When strong leadership is exercised in the operations of such councils, they have the potential to be important vehicles for advocacy and for the coordination of the effective use of resources across the various sectors concerned. However, I know of no examples of such councils being an

important element in any successful reductions of undernutrition.

Immediate Responsibility and Location for Action to Improve Nutrition.   Finally, the location of the immediate activities that are most critical for ensuring that household members are well nourished also may contribute to undernutrition not being treated as a priority by governments. As was noted, these activities are primarily the responsibility of women throughout most of the world, in both developed and developing nations (Sen 1999). The care they provide is an underlying determinant of nutritional status. Although the nurturing role of women finds part of its justification in their physical reproductive capacity, most of the responsibilities women bear in this regard are socially determined. As a consequence, the extent to which women can supply nutritional care depends on their ability to control the allocation of household resources. The importance of gender inequalities in contributing to problems of human development is somewhat more apparent in considering undernutrition than for many other such problems. Where policies and programs remove constraints that limit the respective contributions of men and women to improving nutrition, aggregate nutritional status will improve (Kurz and Johnson-Welch 2001). For instrumental reasons alone —that is, for the technical efficiencies that can be realized—gender analysis should be a necessary component in the design of public policy to reduce levels of undernutrition.

In accounting for how this allocation of responsibility for nutritional care at the household level might be reflected in national policy processes and, in particular, the narratives that contribute to those processes, two hypotheses are suggested. First, improving nutrition may be seen as a women's issue. Because national policy processes are globally dominated by men, efforts to place undernutrition-related problems on policy agendas will be more difficult than seeking public support to address problems relating to male-dominated activities. Second, poor nutrition may be seen as a concern only at the level of the household. That is, in spite of the arguments made earlier, the general attitude might be that poor nutrition is not a public problem that merits a political response. Poorly nourished children may be seen to reflect negatively on the head of their household or, more specifically, on the women who care for them, but not on the broader society and nation. Consequently, the problem may be perceived as not to merit public attention and may thus be excluded from policymaking agendas (Stone, Maxwell, and Keating 2001, 8).

At a more basic level, as was alluded to in the discussion on the importance of narratives in the policy process, the principal challenge in addressing undernutrition as a policy problem is that in most developing nations, a high prevalence of undernutrition in the population is not seen as anomalous and indicative of the inability of the government to fulfill its duties to its citizens. Rather, the citizens themselves seem to accept that undernutrition will be a characteristic of the nation for some time to come, and few voices challenge this assumption. Consequently, in the dominant narratives that motivate policymaking in most developing countries, undernutrition is not identified as being among those problems that the state must address with urgency.

I now turn to the four institutional case studies of nutrition in national policy processes to assess empirically the conceptual understanding of undernutrition (discussed in this and the previous chapter) as a policy problem in developing countries. My objective in doing so is to consider how to overcome the constraints and exploit the opportunities for substantially reducing undernutrition through action in the public sector.

CHAPTER 4

Institutional Study

This chapter describes the project context and motivation for the institutional study and the principal methods used. General information on human and economic development in the four study countries is also provided, offering a broader understanding of the opportunities for, and constraints on, reducing undernutrition in each country's population.

The TANA Project

The institutional study was undertaken in support of a wider effort, the TANA project, which aimed at strengthening and expanding the linkages between nutritionists and agriculturalists, particularly through employing gender-sensitive approaches, to reduce hunger and undernutrition in five countries in Africa—Ghana, Kenya, Mozambique, Nigeria, and Uganda. The project was funded by USAID and implemented between 2001 and 2004 by the International Center for Research on Women, in partnership with IFPRI. The project focused on the problem of barriers to cross-sectoral collaboration between the agriculture and nutrition communities in the project countries that hampered the reduction of poverty, hunger, and malnutrition. The source of the problem was that food security was too often formulated as food production, while nutrition was viewed exclusively as a health issue. This segmented view of agriculture, food, and nutrition inevitably positions these communities as competitors for resources rather than partners in action. The project aimed to work with policymakers, development program planners, and implementers to bridge sectoral gaps, foster increased collaboration, and convert missed opportunities into effective joint action as part of the normal operations of the involved institutions.

The project emerged from a survey of the perceptions of a broad range of experts on the value of and constraints to integrating agriculture and nutrition to address malnutrition (Levin et al. 2003). The dominant opinion expressed by participants in the survey was that the two professional communities are missing important opportunities to collaborate that would have a positive impact on public nutritional well-being. Linking agriculture and nutrition efforts more explicitly would address the frequently observed situation that improved agricultural production or higher rural incomes have not resulted in significant improvements in the nutritional status of rural populations. Moreover, survey participants highlighted the critical need to examine the respective roles of women and men in decisionmaking in the household if malnutrition is to be addressed effectively.

The principal technical focus of the project was on agriculture-based approaches to improved nutrition, approaches that explicitly link the work of agriculturalists with that of nutritionists. These include both direct approaches in agriculture to improve nutrition (breeding crops that have higher levels of micronutrients or promoting nutrient-rich crops, such as vitamin A–rich orange-fleshed sweet potato, for example) and indirect approaches to promote more nutritious diets (in particular, increased income from agricultural production, coupled with improved nutritional knowledge). Although such approaches cannot solve all nutritional problems, they are particularly effective in building and maintaining good nutritional status when malnutrition is related to insufficient food availability and certain micronutrient deficiencies, particularly in agricultural economies.

The project aims were to be attained through the activities of project teams made up of agriculturalists, nutritionists, and gender specialists in each country. The make-up of the project teams in the four countries examined in this report are described in Box 4.1. Each team drafted plans to strengthen the linkages between the nutrition and agriculture sectors in their country and improve the contributions of agricultural programs to nutritional benefits using gender analysis in planning and implementation. The action plans developed by each team typically operated at two levels—the national level and

---

Box 4.1 Institutional Affiliations of the Agriculture–Nutrition Advantage Project Team Members in the Four Study Countries

Ghana:
- Nutrition Unit of the Ghana Health Service (two members)
- Directorate of Crop Services, Ministry of Food and Agriculture
- Directorate of Women in Agricultural Development (WIAD), Ministry of Food and Agriculture
- MOST—The USAID Micronutrient Project
- Food Research Institute
- Crops Research Institute

Mozambique:
- Instituto Nacional de Investigaçào Agronómica (National Institute of Agronomic Research)
- Nutrition Section, Ministry of Health
- Gedlide Institute (national NGO focusing on gender and development)

Nigeria:
- Nutrition Division, Federal Ministry of Health
- Department of Human Nutrition, University of Ibadan
- Department of Home Science and Nutrition, University of Nigeria–Nsukka
- International Institute for Tropical Agriculture
- Department of Agriculture, Oshimili North Local Government Area, Delta State
- Nutrition Unit, Ministry of Health, Borno State
- Department of Rural Development, Federal Ministry of Agriculture and Rural Development
- BASICS II—Nigeria (USAID project)

Uganda:
- National Agricultural Research Organization
- Department of Food Science and Technology, Makerere University (two members)
- National Agricultural Advisory Service (gender specialist)
- AFRICARE, Kabale district (project of an international development NGO)

the local level, where agriculture-based nutritional activities focused on the household were implemented.

For example, the Uganda TANA project team developed a plan of action that was designed to take advantage of the Ugandan government's decentralized decisionmaking process and the emerging Plan for the Modernization of Agriculture (PMA; MAAIF and MFPED 2000) under the Poverty Eradication Action Plan (PEAP; MFPED 2000). This policy environment guided the team's two related sets of activities:

1. Work with farmer groups and other community-based organizations at district and subcounty levels to build knowledge of gender-sensitive agriculture and nutrition interventions and to create demand for support from government agencies for such community-based activities.
2. Raise awareness in executive bodies of the PMA, the steering committee for Uganda's Food and Nutrition Strategy, and district and subcounty governments of the benefits of interventions integrating gender, nutrition, and agriculture.

In addition to funding the activities of the country project teams, several all-country project meetings were held to share experiences and build skills in developing and implementing evidence-based advocacy and in the use of gender analysis in program design and implementation to enhance impact. Through these efforts, the project sought to build the foundation for a network of advocates for linked multisectoral approaches to address undernutrition in Africa. These advocates would ideally be able to engage with policymakers and program implementers (Johnson-Welch, MacQuarrie, and Bunch 2005).

Institutional Study

In addition to the work of the TANA teams in each of the project countries, a key project activity was to undertake the institutional study that forms the empirical basis for this report. The study was motivated by the earlier survey of experts on the value of and constraints to integrating agriculture and nutrition to address malnutrition (Levin et al. 2003). Although there was agreement that the two communities or sectors did not work together effectively, the reason for the failure was not clear. Consequently, in planning the TANA project, an institutional study was included among the project activities to examine institutional and other factors that facilitate or constrain greater partnerships between the two sectors. More specifically, the study was to: (1) assess the extent to which agriculture and nutrition communities work as partners in the four study countries, (2) assess the potential gains from increased collaboration, and (3) determine the various constraints on increased collaboration.

This research was designed to achieve two aims: First, the study was to provide the project teams in the study countries with an objective assessment of the context for their efforts to improve the linkage of agriculture and nutrition in their own countries. The study was to determine whether the implementation of the plans of the project teams may be constrained by institutional factors and whether overlooked opportunities may exist to enhance their impact. Second, the study was to provide more broadly applicable insights on the opportunities and constraints for explicitly linking activities in the two sectors and raising the profile of undernutrition within policy processes operative in other countries. Having identified the barriers to joint action through the study, the project teams would then work to overcome them to build closer partnerships across sectors that would lead to more effective use of resources and to sustained reductions in undernutrition.

The operational definition of institution used in the institutional study was broad. The Oxford English Dictionary includes in its many definitions of the term, "an established law, custom, usage, practice, organization, or other element in the political or social life of a people; a regulative principle or convention subservient to the needs of an organized community or the general ends of civilization" (Oxford University Press 2002). This definition was appropriate for the study. The study was limited to those institutional elements in the study countries that perform (or should perform) key functions in determining whether and how nutritional needs are met at the level of the individual within the household. The institutions studied were primarily those operative at the national level, although both international and local institutions were included. Moreover, both formal and informal institutions were considered. For example, National Committees for Food and Nutrition are formally constituted institutions of a political and administrative nature, whereas the customary roles of men and women in society also constitute an institution—although informal and ideological—in that these customs regulate the way the society is organized. Both of these were among the institutions examined in the institutional study.

The institutional study was carried out in Ghana, Mozambique, Nigeria, and Uganda between mid-2002 and early 2004.[1] The choice of these countries was made primarily to include the different regions of Africa, as well as reflecting some project-specific constraints. However, as discussed later, several important contrasts emerged among these four countries in terms of the nature of their policy processes, the human capacity in nutrition that each country possesses, and the perception of the importance of undernutrition as a policy problem, among others.

Methods

Two qualitative methods were used in the institutional study. First, reviews were undertaken of key primary and secondary documents for each country that focused on food and nutrition, agricultural sector development, and master development planning. Second, semistructured interviews were carried out with 30–40 agriculturalists, nutritionists, and policymakers in each study country.

As the principal scale of analysis in the study is the national level, much of the documentation reviewed for the study had a national perspective or was written for an audience with national responsibilities, and most interviews were conducted in the capital cities with national policymakers and national leaders in agriculture and nutrition. There are two principal reasons for this national focus. First, a key assumption of the TANA project was that broadly improved nutrition is among those goods that national governments are commonly held to be primarily responsible for providing to their citizens (Paarlberg 2002). Second, the resources available for the study were limited. Arranging informant interviews was quite problematic even in the capital cities. Costs would have increased beyond project limits if the study had been extended to consider in-depth district and local level perspectives on the opportunities for and constraints on linking nutrition and agriculture. That said, in all four countries, some information was collected at local levels. However, much more could have been collected.

Document Review. Key documents were collected and reviewed at all stages of the study. These documents included the operative policy documents on food and nutrition and master development planning, where they existed. The key policy statements of interest to the study for each country are listed in Table 4.1. In addition, strategy papers, operational plans, project reports, academic research reports, and journal articles were consulted. Documents were obtained from project team members in the four coun-

---

[1] Although Kenya was a TANA project country, because of budget constraints, only one East African country was selected for the institutional study.

Table 4.1   Key national policy statements for the institutional study

Policy document	Ghana	Mozambique	Nigeria	Uganda
Master development policy	*Ghana Poverty Reduction Strategy 2003–05—An Agenda for Growth and Prosperity* (PRSP)	*PARPA—Action Plan for the Reduction of Absolute Poverty* (PRSP)	None in place at time of study, but *National Economic Empowerment and Development Strategy* completed in 2004	*Poverty Eradication Action Plan* (PRSP)
National nutrition policy	None in place	*Estratégia de Segurança Alimentar e Nutrição* [*National Food Security and Nutrition Strategy*]	*National Policy on Food and Nutrition in Nigeria*	*Uganda Food and Nutrition Policy* (draft submitted to cabinet for approval)
National nutrition action plan	*National Plan of Action on Food and Nutrition, 1995–2000*	*Strategic Plan for Nutrition in Mozambique* (draft) (Nutrition Section of Ministry of Health)	None in place at time of study, but action plan completed in 2003	None in place at time of study, but strategy completed in 2005

Note: PRSP is Poverty Reduction Strategy Paper.

tries, through extensive Internet and library searches before fieldwork, and, where possible, by systematically obtaining key documents from those interviewed.

The focus on the key government policy statements to guide the institutional study can be misleading, because "policy is what it does" (Gillespie, McLachlan, and Shrimpton 2003, 23). That is to say, policy statements are probably not worth the paper they are printed on if they do not result in a reprioritization of government activities and a reallocation of government resources to bring about measurable change in the policy problem they were formulated to address. The documents, in some sense, are an ideal statement of the priorities of government, but the actual priorities are revealed in implementation and allocation of resources. Across the four study countries there are policy statements that do not merit much consideration. However, from the perspective of my interests in this report, even if these key policy statements have not led to changes in priorities or resource allocations, they do reflect the institutional framework in which policy processes operate, the interests of key actors in those processes, and the dominant narratives that frame the problem.

Note that these policy documents are somewhat time bound. In particular, the master development policies considered—generally, Poverty Reduction Strategy Papers (PRSPs)—were drafted with the expectation that each would be revised on a regular basis in a participatory manner to reflect changing social and economic conditions in a country. In the case of Nigeria, no master development policy was in place at the time of the study in 2002, but the National Economic Empowerment and Development Strategy (NEEDS) has since been formulated (NPC 2004). Moreover, these master development frameworks should be expected to change with changes in the ruling regime in each country. The nutrition-oriented policy statements are likely to be more durable, but are also more likely to suffer from irrelevance, along the lines sketched in the previous paragraph, if they result in no reorientation in government effort or allocation of resources.[2]

[2]The impetus for much of the effort to develop national food security and nutrition policies came from the action plans of the 1992 International Conference on Nutrition and the 1996 World Food Summit. The Food and Agri-

Semistructured Interviews. Semistructured interviews with agriculturalists, nutritionists, and policymakers constituted the second method used in the institutional study. These individuals included members of government departments, research organizations, donors, NGOs, and multilateral organizations. Thirty to 40 interviews were carried out in each country.

About 2 weeks were spent conducting interviews in each country. Those in Uganda were conducted during September 5–18, 2002. They took place in the capital, Kampala, or in Entebbe, where the headquarters of the Ministry of Agriculture, Animal Industry, and Fisheries is found, except for a day of interviewing in Luwero District, north of Kampala. The interviews in Mozambique took place between September 26 and October 4, 2002, in Maputo, except for a day of interviewing in Chókwè District in Gaza province. Fieldwork in Nigeria took place during November 14–26, 2002. The first week was spent in the Lagos area, including a day in rural Badagry Local Government Authority of Lagos state, while the second week of interviewing was done in the national capital, Abuja. However, in contrast to the other study countries, where all interviews were done where the subjects lived or worked, several interviewees in Nigeria traveled from other areas of the country to be interviewed. Finally, the Ghana fieldwork took place during March 1–11, 2004.[3] Most of the time was spent in Accra, although 2 days were spent conducting interviews in Cape Coast with regional officers for the Central Region and district officers in Komenda, Edina, Eguafo, Abrem (KEEA) District.

The primary sectoral avenue for identifying key informants for the institutional study was through nutrition. The nutrition community in the study countries is considerably smaller than that of agriculture. A more manageable study was made possible by limiting the range of informants to those whose work explicitly involved nutritional issues, could be expected to touch on nutrition-related issues, or whose qualifications included some nutritional expertise. As a consequence, although the study was developed to examine linkages between agriculture and nutrition, from an agricultural perspective, the study is limited to those few areas where the agricultural sector is concerned with nutrition. However, the agricultural and, hence, food orientation of the study likely limited the understanding of some important policy perspectives on health and care as determinants of improved nutritional status and on the broader role of the health sector in addressing undernutrition in each country.

Interviewees were initially selected by asking the project team members in each country to identify the individuals who perform certain institutional functions regarding nutrition in the public sector. In responding to this initial request, the country team members suggested additional likely useful interviewees in each country. Finally, once the interviews were underway, respondents suggested other individuals for interviews—a nonrandom "snowball" sample selection method (Henry 1990, 21). Moreover, as the fieldwork was done sequentially in the four countries, experience from fieldwork in previous countries guided the selection of key informants. Table 4.2 disaggre-

---

culture Organization of the United Nations and the World Health Organization have provided assistance in the formulation of such policies to many developing countries.

[3]The institutional study was designed in 2002 to be a three-country study—Uganda, Mozambique, and Nigeria—one country from each of East, Southern, and West Africa. However, after fieldwork was completed in the three countries and an initial report written, additional resources were made available to undertake the same study in Ghana. Prior commitments resulted in the Ghana fieldwork being delayed until more than a year after the fieldwork in the other three countries had been completed.

Table 4.2   Institutional characteristics of interviewees for the institutional study

Scope	Ghana		Mozambique		Nigeria		Uganda	
	National	Local	National	Local	National	Local	National	Local
Nutrition and health								
Government agency	7	3	3	1	4	4	2	1
Research	6	0	1	0	5	0	3	0
Donor	3	0	0	0	4	0	2	0
NGO	5	1	3	0	1	1	2	0
Subtotal	21	4	7	1	14	5	9	1
Total	25	8	19	10				
Agriculture								
Government agency	2	3	4	1	4	2	7	1
Research	0	0	5	0	1	0	2	0
Donor	1	0	5	0	2	0	1	0
NGO	0	0	1	0	0	0	2	1
Subtotal	3	3	15	1	7	2	12	2
Total	6	16	9	14				
Other sector								
Government agency	4	1	2	0	3	0	5	2
Research	0	0	3	0	0	0	1	0
Donor	0	0	4	0	0	0	4	0
NGO	1	0	6	1	0	0	0	0
Subtotal	5	1	15	1	3	0	10	2
Total	6		16		3		12	
Total number of interviewees	37		40		31		36	

Note: NGO is nongovernmental organization.

gates the interviewees in each country by institutional affiliations according to sector, public or private sector, and national or local standing. An institutional listing of those interviewed is provided in Appendix A.

Given their selection process, the interviewees as a group do not provide an unbiased representation of the spectrum of opinions in each country on the significance of undernutrition as a policy problem, on how nutrition fits into policy processes, or on the degree to which multisectoral action could be taken to assist the undernourished. Moreover, most respondents were based in the national capital and so had limited recent experience with nutrition issues at regional or local levels. The pattern that emerges in Table 4.2 closely reflects both particular features of the context of nutrition in the public sector and possible bias in interviewee selection.

One source of bias is in the composition of the TANA project team in each study country and, in particular, who in that team provided most local direction in the implementation of the institutional study. In both Ghana and Nigeria, nutritionists constituted the majority on the project team, and the agriculture sector had no specific mandates on nutrition issues except that the agriculture extension service was responsible for disseminating nutrition information to women in farming households. Consequently, the distribution of interviewees across the sectors in these two countries favors nutritionists and the health sector. In Mozambique, there are very few nutritionists in the public sector, and any coordination on nutrition issues across sectors is managed by the Ministry of Agriculture. Consequently, the individuals interviewed in Mozambique are disproportionately agriculturalists or from other sectors than nutrition. The strong reliance on international NGOs in Mozambique for the provision of public services is reflected in the large proportion of interviewees there who are categorized as being in other sectors than nutrition or agriculture. Finally, in Uganda, the composition of the project team enabled stronger links to be developed with agriculturalists than with nutritionists, although in many cases the agriculturalists interviewed were responsible for some nutrition-related activities. Moreover, gender analysis (as a tool to guide policy formulation and program design) and decentralized government administration are both more advanced in Uganda than in the other study countries. Consequently, most of the Ugandan interviewees categorized as being in other sectors are either specialists in gender analysis or local government administrators.

Guides were prepared for the interviews conducted during the fieldwork. A close review of the documentation obtained before the fieldwork was done provided the basis for the content of the interviews. The interview guides for Mozambique, Nigeria, and Uganda are very similar, only being modified to better reflect the particular policy environments and instiutional organization of the public sector in each country. This common interview guide is presented in Appendix B with notes on where country-specific text was used. Although the general format of the guide for Ghana was the same, some questions were dropped and others added as a result of the initial analysis of the other three study countries. The Ghana guide is presented in Appendix C.

The interviews were relatively unstructured. The guides were used to make sure that all relevant study points within the expertise of the interviewee were covered, time allowing, and were used as guides rather than questionnaires. Most interviews were conducted with individuals alone, the preferred method, and typically lasted 1 hour. All interviews were conducted in English, except for two in Mozambique that required Portuguese–English translation.[4] Usually a research associate and I jointly conducted the interviews, and we both took detailed notes. I was present at 80 percent of the interviews. The two sets of notes from the interviews were transcribed the same day, in most cases.

For this report, only selected portions of the information gathered through the document review and the semistructured interviews are used. In contrast to the institutional study for the TANA project, the focus here is not so strongly on agriculture or gender, although both still feature as inherent issues in improving nutrition in Sub-Saharan Africa. Rather, my aim is to use selectively the information gathered to understand what it is about policymaking at the national level, nutrition, and nutrition within policymaking that makes it difficult for undernutrition to be targeted as a national development priority in the four study countries. Although nutrition concerns guided the institutional study for the TANA project, here I concentrate even more narrowly on nutrition as a policy problem.

Finally, I should clarify the time bounds of the perspectives gained on nutrition within policy processes in each country. As noted, the fieldwork in Mozambique, Nigeria, and Uganda was completed in late 2002,

---

[4]However, documentation in both Portuguese and English was examined for the study in Mozambique.

while that in Ghana was completed in early 2004. For the most part, the analysis for Ghana and Mozambique reflects the situation in those countries observed at the time of the fieldwork. However, subsequent work by me in Uganda and Nigeria has permitted further consideration of how undernutrition is addressed as a development problem in the two countries.[5]

Study Countries

In this section, general overviews are provided on each study country before comparisons are made on key characteristics related to nutrition, socioeconomic development, and governance.

Ghana.   Ghana has made significant progress in social and economic development over the past 10–15 years and has begun to achieve some of the potential noted when it became among the first countries in Africa to achieve independence from colonial rule 50 years ago. Although considerably smaller, Ghana is similar to Nigeria in agroclimatic and, to a lesser degree, social terms. Agriculture is the mainstay of the livelihoods of most Ghanaian households. Generally, Ghana is considered food secure, although the sharp seasonality of rainfall in the north leads to annual periods of food insecurity there.

However, Ghana has seen erratic trends in the prevalence of stunted children in recent years, with a decline of 6 percent between 1993 and 1998, but a gain of more than 6 percent between 1998 and 2003. Of children less than 3 years of age, 26.7 percent were stunted (low height for age) in their growth in 2003. Underweight (low weight for age) prevalence among this group has declined consistently, if slowly, since 1988. Infant and child mortality levels are the lowest and life expectancy at birth is the highest of the four countries. In Ghana,

there are important regional contrasts in child malnutrition. Prevalence of child stunting in rural areas is 60 percent higher than what is found in urban areas. The three northern regions of the country have stunting prevalence rates of about 40 percent on average, whereas in the other regions of the country, the prevalence is at least 10 percent lower.

Ghana has experienced long periods of poor governance, but unlike Nigeria, has not undergone violent upheavals and civil strife as a consequence. Kwame Nkrumah led Ghana to independence from Britain in 1957. Having embarked on a relatively unsuccessful course of economic development through industrialization, he was overthrown by the military in 1966. The following 15 years were characterized by coups and unsuccessful attempts to develop a viable political system for the country. In 1981, J. J. Rawlings led his second successful military coup in 3 years, but this time remained in power and adopted conservative, free market economic policies in line with the structural adjustment reforms being advocated by the International Monetary Fund and the World Bank. The economy has grown quite consistently since the mid-1980s. Average annual per capita GDP growth was 2.4 percent between 2000 and 2004. Foreign investment levels have been relatively high, particularly in the mineral sector.

Democratic government was reintroduced in 1992, when Rawlings successfully ran for president as a civilian in multiparty elections. He won again in 1996. Constitutionally barred from running in 2000, his political party lost the presidency to John Kufuor. Kufuor retained the presidency in elections held in late 2004. Additionally, between 1988 and 1993, important government decentralization laws were passed. These included the institution of democrati-

---

[5]In Uganda, this engagement remained particularly close, as it included participation in the formulation of the Uganda Food and Nutrition Strategy (MAAIF and MOH 2005).

cally elected District Assemblies in all 110 districts.

Generally, Ghana is acknowledged to be a country in which an optimistic outlook on the economy and the political system is warranted. Although there is considerable political debate at the national level, it respects the political institutions now in place. The country has enjoyed relative economic stability in recent years and has been experiencing broad-based economic growth with a declining prevalence of poverty. Although the rural areas have not benefited from this economic growth to the degree that urban centers have, even in rural areas the trends are encouraging. However, noneconomic indicators of development, such as the mixed child nutrition indicators noted earlier, suggest that a firm developmental trend is not yet established.

Mozambique.   Mozambique runs along the Indian Ocean coast for 2,500 km in southeastern Africa. Its total population is about 20 million, 68 percent of whom reside in rural areas. Agriculture accounts for 80 percent of all employment. Mozambique has a single rainy season between October and April. Subsistence food crops, notably maize and cassava, dominate agricultural production. Cashew and cotton are important cash crops, with tobacco and pigeonpea increasing in significance. There remain large tracts of unexploited arable land, particularly in the north.

Although Mozambique is endowed with considerable agricultural resources, the country is considered food insecure. In the early 1990s, drought and insecurity at the end of the civil war caused major food shortages requiring a large international food aid response. Both floods and cyclones devastate stretches of coastline and their hinterlands every few years, destroying crops and infrastructure. Although crop production can be good in some areas and at the same time poor in others, the geography of the country makes it difficult to move food from productive areas to those of deficit. In-

formation on where food is needed often does not get to areas of supply in a timely fashion. Transport links are tenuous, as the north–south orientation of the country means that most roads have to cross the rivers draining the interior. The frequent floods destroy bridges on these rivers. Making sure that all areas of the country have adequate food remains a preoccupation of the Mozambican government.

Undernutrition is a problem. Of children less than 3 years of age, 37 percent are stunted and 26 percent are underweight. Rates are about 15 percent higher for both measures in rural areas compared to urban settings. HIV infection also is a more significant problem for Mozambique than for the other study countries: more than 16 percent of adults are infected.

Mozambique attained independence from Portugal in 1975 after more than a decade of armed struggle led by FRELIMO. A centrally planned, socialist economic system was established. Shortly after independence, the RENAMO rebellion began, particularly in the central provinces of the country. This civil war led to hundreds of thousands of deaths, decimated the country's infrastructure, and set back the development prospects of Mozambique for the duration of the conflict. Exhaustion with the war and the change of government in South Africa, RENAMO's principal supporter, provided the necessary conditions for a peace treaty to be negotiated and signed in 1992. FRELIMO retained power after competitive multiparty presidential and legislative elections in 1994 in which RENAMO was the main challenger. Subsequent national elections have been held in 1999 and 2005, with the ruling party retaining power.

In 1987, the Mozambican government began altering its earlier course of a centrally planned and controlled economic system and instituted broad reforms to create an economy based on private initiative and free market forces. With the attainment of peace, this reform process intensified.

Poverty reduction through sustained rapid and broad-based economic growth is now the principal policy priority for the government. Encouraging macrolevel results from these reforms have been seen in recent years, with annual economic growth averaging more than 6 percent in the latter half of the 1990s. Relative to other countries in Africa, Mozambique has captured a substantial amount of foreign investment. As a consequence of this good performance, Mozambique is held up in international development circles as an African example of the successes of consistent, market-oriented policies. In a rough, subjective ranking of the study countries based on this standard, it stands slightly below Uganda and Ghana, and well above Nigeria.

However, a critical constraint on the effective operation of the Mozambican state in meeting its development goals is its lack of professionals. This deficiency is a result both of its colonial history, during which the Portuguese provided few avenues for training to indigenous Mozambicans, and conditions in the years after independence, when building human capacity was not a priority as the state struggled to survive the civil war. Moreover, with so few professionals available in the country, the government has difficulty retaining staff as it competes with the private sector and NGOs, as well as with the labor market in neighboring South Africa.

Nigeria.   Nigeria is a heterogeneous country. The country straddles most of the agroclimatic zones of West Africa, except the driest. Socially, it is divided by religion, language (with more than 250 languages), and complex patterns of ethnicity. Although oil drives the economy, the largest occupational class for Nigerians is farming. Even so, the country has some of the largest cities in Sub-Saharan Africa.

The general assumption is that Nigeria is food secure at the national level, in that sufficient food is produced and is generally available for the needs of the population. When poor weather conditions for agriculture occur, they tend to be localized to an agroecological zone at most. If the pearl millet or sorghum harvest in the north fails, for example, it is unlikely that the cassava, yam, or maize harvests farther south will be much affected. Although there is considerable room for improvement, Nigeria has an adequate transport system and an active commercial sector that can move food from areas of surplus to those of deficit. Availability of food rarely is seen to be a problem. At the national level, this characteristic of the country reduces the political importance of food and, by extension, nutrition issues.

However, the statistics on child nutritional status available for Nigeria stand in contrast to the general assumption of Nigeria as being relatively food secure. Of children less than 3 years of age, 36 percent were found to be stunted and 29 percent underweight in the 2003 Nigeria Demographic and Health Survey. Although Nigeria has the physical and human resources to raise standards of living significantly, the challenge of broad human development has not been effectively addressed and remains large.

Nigeria gained its independence from Great Britain in 1960. The first in a long sequence of military coups took place in 1966. Lieutenant-General Olusegun Obasanjo, as military leader, oversaw a transition back to civilian rule in 1979. The second period of civilian rule lasted less than 5 years. Fifteen years of rule by various generals ended in 1999 with Obasanjo, running as a civilian, being elected president. In 2003, he was reelected to serve a second and final term in office.

Obasanjo's presidency has not been overwhelmingly successful, and the road out of economic and political crisis for Nigeria remains long and difficult. The political tension that has characterized Nigeria since the end of colonial rule remains high. Broad-based economic growth remains elusive. There is little evidence that poverty is declining. Although food is available, access to food for many Nigerian households has become more difficult in past decades. Nevertheless, the current democratic system of government retains considerable support and generally is viewed as a superior, more hopeful choice than a return to military rule.

Uganda. Uganda is a relatively small and densely populated land-locked country straddling the equator north and west of Lake Victoria in eastern Africa. The total population of Uganda is 26 million, with more than 85 percent residing in rural areas. The more productive southern half of the country has two rainy seasons a year. Population densities in this area commonly are more than 100 persons per km^2. The food economy in the south is primarily based on *matooke* (cooking banana), with livestock also being important in some areas. In the drier areas of the north, there is only one rainy season, and population densities are considerably lower. Here the food economy is more diverse, based on cereals and livestock. Agriculture is the source of employment for 80 percent of the rural population in Uganda. Although smallholder cash cropping of coffee, cotton, and tobacco is relatively common, subsistence food crop production continues to dominate agriculture.

The general consensus is that Uganda is food secure. Farmers produce enough food to satisfy the requirements of the population, except in areas where armed opposition groups are active. Uganda has a relatively benign climate and productive soils. Although there is considerable room for increased efficiencies in the marketing system, outside the areas of conflict, it is felt that the food crop marketing system can effectively provide food to areas facing food production shortfalls.

Nevertheless, undernutrition is a problem, with both protein-energy and micronutrient undernutrition more common than is widely perceived. The Uganda 2006 Demographic and Health Survey found that 28 percent of children younger than 3 were stunted and 23 percent were underweight.

Moreover, the percentage of individuals with a level of consumption below a basic-needs poverty line is 39 percent in rural areas and 10 percent in urban centers.

Uganda gained its independence from Great Britain in 1962. After a military coup in 1971, 15 years of misrule, economic decline, and civil war followed. In 1986, the insurgent National Resistance Army captured Kampala and installed Yoweri Museveni as head of state. As their power was consolidated, important political reforms were introduced to increase representation in public life across all sectors of society, although the formation of political parties was restricted. Strong efforts have been made to decentralize government to establish local control for managing local issues. The government has been able to pursue aggressive, creative policies and strategies for economic development and poverty reduction.

However, the government's control of Uganda is not absolute. Most significantly, for two decades, a rebellion in the north has proven surprisingly difficult to put down, displacing large numbers of people and exacerbating food insecurity and malnutrition. Other rebellions have sprung up in the past in the southwest. The northeastern border zone has always been an area of insecurity. Most of these armed opposition groups do not have an articulate political stance, so it is difficult to characterize them as emerging from dissatisfaction with the policies of the Ugandan government. Nevertheless, they have diverted the attention of the state and have the potential to weaken it.

Comparisons of Study Countries. In this section, the national-level statistics presented in Table 4.3 are examined to establish some degree of comparability among the four study countries. However, there are important regional differences in all four countries that are masked by these national statistics. For example, the north of Uganda is an area of longstanding insecurity, where, consequently, food security and prospects for economic growth are undermined. The

Table 4.3 Selected national indicators of social and economic development

Indicator	Ghana	Mozambique	Nigeria	Uganda
Land area (km²)	227,540	784,090	910,770	197,100
Population (millions, mid-2006 estimate)	22.6	19.9	134.5	27.7
Rural population (percent of total)	56	68	56	88
Nutrition, child survival, and health				
Stunted, age less than 3 years/annual trend since previous DHS (percent who are low height for age)[a]	26.7/+6.7	36.7/+0.8	35.8/–9.7	28.1/–7.4
Underweight, age less than 3 years/annual trend since previous DHS (percent who are low weight for age)	23.5/–1.4	25.7/–0.4	29.3/+2.0	23.1/–1.6
Infant mortality (deaths of infants aged less than 1 year per 1,000 live births)	59	108	100	81
HIV infection prevalence in adults (percent, 15–49 years old)	2.3	16.1	3.9	6.7
Life expectancy at birth (years)	57	42	44	47
Improved drinking water sources (percent of population using)	75	43	48	60
Adequate sanitation facilities (percent of population using)	18	32	44	43
Food security and agriculture				
Calories per capita per day from domestic supply (mean 1999–2003)	2,615	2,030	2,714	2,351
Food aid, cereals, all donors (thousand metric tons, annual mean 1998–2002)	68.9	205.0	3.1	74.1
Human capacity				
Illiteracy (percent of population aged 15 years and older)	46	54	33	31
Illiteracy—male/female (percent)	37/54	38/69	26/41	21/41
Educational attainment—persons aged 20–29 years who have completed at least 9 years of schooling (percent)	53.6	8.1	45.7	23.1
Sex differences in secondary school (female as percentage of male enrollment)	85	69	82	78
Economic performance, poverty, and inequality				
GDP per capita (PPP US$, 2004)	$2,240	$1,240	$1,154	$1,478
GDP growth (annual percent, mean 2000–2004)	4.7	7.6	5.1	5.7
GDP per capita growth (annual percent, mean 2000–2004)	2.4	5.4	2.7	2.3
Foreign aid per capita (mean 2000–2004)	$40.17	$67.13	$2.53	$34.15
Poverty headcount (percentage of population consuming <US$1.00 per day/<US$2.00 per day, PPP)	44.8/78.5	37.9/78.4	70.2/90.8	36.9/n.a.
Inequality (percentage of all consumption by poorest 20 percent/ wealthiest 20 percent of population)	5.6/46.6	6.5/46.5	4.4/55.7	5.9/49.7
Inequality (Gini coefficient)	39.6	39.6	50.6	43.0
Estimates of governance, 2005[b]				
Voice and accountability	+0.41	–0.06	–0.69	–0.59
Political stability	+0.16	+0.04	–1.77	–1.32
Government effectiveness	–0.09	–0.34	–0.92	–0.48
Regulatory quality	–0.14	–0.60	–1.01	+0.01
Rule of law	–0.23	–0.72	–1.38	–0.74
Control of corruption	–0.38	–0.68	–1.22	–0.87

Sources: Filmer (2005); FAO (2006); Kaufmann, Kraay, and Mastruzzi (2006); Population Reference Bureau (2006); UNDP (2006); World Bank (2006b).

Notes: DHS is Demographic and Health Survey; GDP is gross domestic product; n.a. is not available; PPP is purchasing power parity.

[a]Year of latest DHS: Ghana, 2003; Mozambique, 2003; Nigeria, 2003; and Uganda, 2006.

[b]Relative ranking of 175 countries over six dimensions; scale –2.5 to 2.5; mean of 0.

northern areas of both Nigeria and Ghana perform poorly on most social indicators relative to the rest of these countries. In all four countries, there are sharp differences between rural and urban areas in economic growth and welfare improvements in recent years. Such changes in rural areas are slow or nonexistent. Nevertheless, although the statistics are not wholly consistent, broad patterns can be detected.

Concerning the nutritional status of their populations, the countries are rather similar. The incidence of child underweight is comparable and relatively high across the four. Stunting levels in Ghana are somewhat less than in Mozambique and Nigeria, but recent trends there are discouraging. The most recent nutritional survey for Uganda notably saw a welcome drop in stunting among children less than 3, although prevalence levels remain high. The infant mortality rates are relatively consistent with the statistics on child anthropometry.

The data confirm assumptions that Mozambique is somewhat food insecure, while Uganda, Nigeria, and Ghana are more secure. Using an average daily per capita recommended consumption value of 2,000 calories, figures from the Food and Agriculture Organization of the United Nations show domestic production in Uganda, Nigeria, and Ghana to be above that value, with Nigeria and Ghana well above it. Mozambique, in contrast, has only attained this level of calorie availability in the past few years. This statistic reflects the availability of food and not access by the population to that food, so is only indicative of aggregate food security status. However, the large food aid shipments that Mozambique continues to receive annually support a view that its aggregate food security remains vulnerable.

Using illiteracy and educational attainment as indicators of the quality of human capital available in each country, Mozambique stands out with its low levels. More than half of Mozambican adults cannot read, and very few young adults have more than a primary education. In contrast, in the other study countries, only about one-third of adults cannot read. In all four countries, there are significant differences in the levels of illiteracy between women and men. With regard to educational attainment, in Ghana and Nigeria, although the data are not wholly consistent with that for literacy, secondary education is more the norm than the exception.

Assessing the four countries on broad economic standing shows Ghana performing the best overall, with the highest level of per capita GDP, at least half again higher than the other study countries. However, the figures for prevalence of poverty in Ghana are higher than would be expected with this level of economic production. Although on a per capita basis, Mozambique's economy has not attained the size of Uganda's, the trends are favorable, with the strongest economic growth of the four countries. Poverty headcount rates based on a $1.00/day purchasing power parity (PPP) poverty line are only slightly higher in Mozambique than in Uganda and are actually lower than in Ghana. All three countries receive substantial amounts of foreign aid, reflecting both apparent need and evaluations of the countries' development prospects by donors.

Nigeria, in contrast, presents a mixed economic performance. Nigeria's GDP per capita is similar to that of Mozambique. Trends in economic growth have been erratic. Nigeria experienced negative per capita growth in the late 1990s, but has seen improvements since then, particularly as its oil sector has benefited from higher prices and its macroeconomic management has improved. Poverty is exceptionally high, to such an extent that the validity of the statistics or the methods underlying them is questionable. Inequality is also high, with the wealthiest quintile of the population accounting for more than half of all consumption. Nigeria receives very little international development assistance, reflecting both the rich resource base of the country and the governance problems.

Table 4.4   Matrix of the development, policy, and institutional context for nutrition across study countries

Issue	Ghana	Mozambique	Nigeria	Uganda
Scale	Similar in many ways to Uganda. Lower population density, greater urbanization.	Almost as large as Nigeria, but much less densely populated.	Large population. Politically complex and unstable. Not very comparable to other study countries.	Relatively densely populated. Smaller than other study countries.
Economic development	Highest gross domestic product per capita of all study countries. Economy is growing. Declines in poverty through the 1990s.	Has put in place much of what is necessary for sustainable, broad economic growth. Impressive development, if from very low base.	Sustainable, broad-based economic development elusive. Oil is economic foundation, benefits of which are enjoyed by a small portion of the population.	Making progress in economic development, experiencing sustained economic growth. Mixed achievements in poverty reduction.
Policymaking processes	Policy important to government, but policymaking process is less formal and closely defined than in Uganda and Mozambique.	Technocratic planning mechanisms quite important in guiding its economic path.	Rather ineffectual planning. Generally disordered, personalized policy environment, reflecting political complexity of country. Technical inputs to policy debates given less weight than in other countries.	Formal, closely defined, and relatively transparent policymaking processes in place, with close oversight and engagement by the president. Relies on technical assessments of policy options.
Professional human resources	Relatively large numbers of trained Ghanaians. Poor incentive structures for professionals within Ghana. Brain drain to developed countries.	Exceptionally thin. Efforts to build capacity hampered in past. In nutrition, lack of capacity especially striking.	Large numbers of trained individuals, but very poor use being made of them in public sector. Hundreds of masters-level trained nutritionists.	Constraints posed by insufficient expertise in country less critical than in Mozambique. Decentralization of government has increased demand.
Nutrition as policy	In all four countries, low priority given nutrition in the policymaking arena. Frameworks for nutrition activities neglected or still being developed; considerable room for improvement. Nutrition activities principally funded by international donors.			

Governance can be defined as "the traditions and institutions by which authority in a country is exercised," and includes how governments are selected and monitored, the quality and process of policymaking, and the respect accorded the economic and social institutions of government by both the state and its citizens (Kaufmann, Kraay, and Zoido-Lobatón 2002, 4). As governance concerns are an important part of the institutional analysis of this study, the final rows in Table 4.3 provide some comparable, if imperfect, indicators of the relative quality of governance in the study countries. Ghana and Mozambique show relatively higher levels of quality of governance. However, as almost all measures for the study countries are below the international mean of zero, there is room for improvement—particularly in Nigeria.

Although difficult to capture empirically, the four countries can be assessed on the strength of their mechanisms of policy process in a somewhat subjective manner. Drawn from the fieldwork and background reading for the institutional study, qualitative descriptions are presented in Table 4.4. The importance of technically sound and explicit policy formulation to guide government actions and resource allocations differs among the countries, being most important in Uganda. Similarly, the ability to implement the policies developed and thus the quality of public services also differs among countries. However, none of the study countries has overcome all, or even many, of the challenges to effective public provision of nutrition-related goods and services. The continuing high levels of child undernutrition in all four of the study countries are evidence of the lack of government success in this regard.

In this chapter, I described the TANA project and its institutional study, which provided the materials for the analysis presented in this report. General contextual information was also provided on the four study countries. In the next chapter, I examine the degree to which undernutrition is addressed as a national policy problem in each country. In particular, I consider the policymaking institutions that are (or could be) involved in formulating policies to reduce undernutrition, the actors engaged in developing or implementing such policies, the narratives used to raise the priority of undernutrition in policymaking, and those circumstances that may help focus state attention on the problem of undernutrition.

CHAPTER 5

Nutrition in National Policy Processes in Ghana, Mozambique, Nigeria, and Uganda

In Chapter 2, the policy process was broken down into four elements—structures, actors, narratives, and timing. In this chapter, the place of nutrition in the policies that are used to prioritize public action and allocate state resources is examined by considering how nutrition is treated by these four elements in each country in turn. These are examined following a description of the place of nutrition in the public sector in each country, the policies that guide the government in addressing undernutrition, and the level of resources allocated to such action. This chapter concludes with a brief assessment of the important differences and commonalities among the four countries in the treatment of undernutrition in national policy processes.

Nutrition-focused institutions and policy documents that are similar in name (and often in make-up) are found in all four countries. In presenting the individual country case studies, this similarity can make cross-country comparisons confusing. Table 5.1 helps clarify some of these elements across the four countries.

Ghana

Nutrition in the Public Sector in Ghana

Nutrition in Ghana is strongly associated with the health sector. The Nutrition Unit of the Ghana Health Service has principal oversight on nutrition at the national level for the government of Ghana, and is located institutionally within the Public Health Division of the Service. The Nutrition Unit primarily has a technical orientation. The head of the Unit is responsible for general administration and for acquiring funding for programs carried out by the Unit. In addition, national-level coordinators for six programs work in the Unit—vitamin A, anemia, iodine, infant feeding, supplementary feeding, and a nutrition-focused community poverty reduction project.

The Nutrition Unit also has responsibility for a decentralized system of nutrition service provision. A regional nutrition officer is posted in each Regional Health Service in the ten regions of Ghana. These individuals are responsible for planning, facilitating, and monitoring the implementation of all nutrition programs carried out by the Ghana Health Service in the region. Each regional nutrition officer reports both to the head of the Nutrition Unit in Accra and to the regional director of health services for their region. In turn, the regional nutrition officers provide support and guidance to the district nutrition officers in most of the 110 districts of the country. The district nutrition officers report both to their district director of health and to their regional nutrition officer. Funds for carrying out nutrition activities in the districts come through the Ghana Health Service and, potentially, from allocations by district assemblies.

Table 5.1 Key institutions and policies related to nutrition activities in the study countries

Issue	Ghana	Mozambique	Nigeria	Uganda
Location of nutrition policy oversight in government	No such institution established. The Nutrition Unit of the Ghana Health Service has principal oversight and leads most technical activities in nutrition in Ghana, but with little formal coordination with other sectors.	Secretariado Técnico de Segurança Alimentar e Nutrição (SETSAN), the national food security and nutrition secretariat, is housed in the Ministry of Agriculture and Rural Development. Its membership includes government ministries, public agencies, and nongovernmental organizations involved in nutrition and food security.	National Committee on Food and Nutrition (NCFN) is located in the National Planning Commission. Its membership includes government agencies involved in nutrition, as well as academic experts.	Uganda Food and Nutrition Council (UFNC) is a multi-sectoral body housed in the secretariat for the Plan for Modernisation of Agriculture (PMA) in the Ministry of Finance, Planning, and Economic Development.
National nutrition policy	No policy document on nutrition developed. The *Ghana National Plan of Action on Food and Nutrition, 1995–2000* is closest thing to such a policy document, but was not being used at the time of fieldwork.	*Estratégia de Segurança Alimentar e Nutrição [National Food Security and Nutrition Strategy]*. A separate strategic plan for nutrition was in draft form at the time of fieldwork. This document was prepared for the Nutrition Section of the Ministry of Health.	*National Policy on Food and Nutrition.* A linked strategy for the implementation of this policy was written after the fieldwork.	*Uganda Food and Nutrition Policy.* A linked strategy for the implementation of this policy was written after the fieldwork.
National master development plan	*Ghana Poverty Reduction Strategy* (GPRS)	*Plano de Acção para a Redução da Pobreza Absoluta* (PARPA; *Action Plan for the Reduction of Absolute Poverty*)	No such plan was in place at the time of the fieldwork. In 2004, the *National Economic Empowerment and Development Strategy* (NEEDS) was published.	*Poverty Eradication Action Plan* (PEAP)

Outside the health sector, the Ministry of Food and Agriculture has the greatest number of staff working on nutrition issues, predominantly within the Women in Agricultural Development (WIAD) department. It is among the smallest of the eight technical directorates of the Ministry, with fewer than 10 technical staff members at the national level. Its activities focus on nutrition and food security, kitchen and farm demon-stration programs, gender and HIV/AIDS, and value-addition through postharvest processing. Most of the technical staff are women trained in nutrition or home science. In undertaking this work, WIAD works relatively closely with the Ghana Health Service Nutrition Unit.

WIAD undertakes its activities with farming households through the staff of the Department of Agricultural Extension Services using a training-and-visit extension system. Nutrition or other WIAD information is conveyed to the field-level extension staff through a training-of-trainers structure, whereby the national WIAD staff members train regional agricultural officers responsible for WIAD activities who, in turn, train district agricultural development officers who have special WIAD responsibilities. These district officers then train the field extension staff and provide technical backstopping to them as they disseminate the information to farmers and farming households.[1]

Nutrition-oriented activities are also found in the education sector. Nutrition is one of the components of the Life Skills home science and health curriculum taught in junior secondary schools by the Ghana Education Service, as well as being part of the School Health Education Programme to promote the health knowledge of primary and secondary school students. The University of Ghana at Legon, near Accra, provides undergraduate and graduate training in nutrition through the Department of Nutrition and Food Science. Although the training has a strong clinical orientation, courses are taught, and several of the faculty members are carrying out research in community nutrition. The University of Development Studies in Tamale, Northern Region, also offers an undergraduate degree in Community Nutrition, the orientation of which is field-focused rather than clinical. The University also hosts a Food and Nutrition Security Unit that undertakes community-based research and provides short-course training on applied food and nutrition security topics, most notably to district officers. Nutrition also is taught at several professional training schools, such as the health training institutes. In 2003, the Ghana Health Service, working with the USAID-funded LINKAGES project, reviewed and strengthened the nutrition component of the curricula used in its medical and paramedical training institutes.

Several Ghanaian and international NGOs, often working with local government agencies, carry out food security activities that also involve nutrition, particularly in the north of Ghana. The population in the north regularly experiences seasonal food insecurity and, partly as a consequence, has the highest prevalence of malnourished children in the country. Moreover, at the time of the Ghana fieldwork in 2004, several child survival programs supported by USAID worked in close collaboration, in particular, with the Nutrition Unit of the Ghana Health Service—the LINKAGES project on infant nutrition, the Basic Support for Institutionalizing Child Survival II (BASICS II) project on the integrated management of childhood illnesses, and the USAID Micronutrient Program (MOST) for vitamin A supplementation and anemia control. Finally, UNICEF and the World Health Organization, the agencies of the United Nations for children and health, respectively, support interventions to reduce malnutrition in Ghana. UNICEF devotes resources for work that focuses on child and maternal nutrition, micronutrient-deficiency control, and household food security in several pilot districts in the north. The World Health Organization works primarily in partnership with the Ghana Health Service on a broad range of health issues, including nutrition through child survival and initiatives on the integrated management of childhood illness, anemia control, and vitamin A supplementation.

With regard to building and sustaining sufficient professional expertise in human nutrition, Ghana is relatively well served.

---

[1]Unfortunately, the design of this nutrition extension program in the agricultural sector is gender-blind, with predominantly male agricultural extension staff being responsible for conveying nutritional information to the women who are the primary nutritional caregivers in farming households. There are no indications that the inherent gender barriers are effectively bridged when discussing such topics as food preparation, infant care, and breastfeeding.

The Department of Nutrition and Food Science at the University of Ghana annually has about 100 undergraduate and 35 graduate students enrolled. Although many of these students will follow a career path in food science in the private sector or pursue further training abroad, others will work at the national or regional level in nutrition in the Ghana Health Service or with NGOs. The program in community nutrition at the University of Development Studies in Tamale also provides bachelors-level training. Professional training for district officers is provided through a 3-year diploma-course in community health at the Rural Health Training School in Kintampo. For the current level of programming in public nutrition in Ghana, existing training programs in human nutrition are adequate. However, it is important to highlight the severe problem of emigration of trained professionals that Ghana experiences. Nutritionists are not immune to the attractions of more remunerative work elsewhere and are a part of this brain drain.

To guide the funding of public nutrition programs, the government of Ghana has no approved policy on nutrition to establish prioritization among the various concerned government sectors and public agencies or the allocation of financial resources. The only formal government statement specifically focusing on nutrition, the Ghana National Plan of Action on Food and Nutrition 1995–2000, was developed as an outcome of the International Conference on Nutrition held in Rome in December 1992 (GOG 1995). The action plan was developed by a multisectoral team led by the deputy minister for Health, under the patronage of the minister of Food and Agriculture. Although some of the language and content of the National Plan of Action appears in later broader policies on human development, such as the Ghana Poverty Reduction Strategy (GPRS; GOG 2003), the document itself is dated and is not used to guide or justify resource allocations by government.

Consequently, the funding acquired from government by the Nutrition Unit for technical programs is done through the routine annual budgeting process. This process entails the head of the Nutrition Unit submitting a budget request for the Unit as part of the negotiations through which the Public Health Division formulates its overall budget request alongside those of other divisions of the Ghana Health Service. The resultant negotiated Ghana Health Service budget request is taken by the Ministry of Health to the Ministry of Finance and Economic Planning and considered alongside the budget requests of other Ministries. At each step of the budgeting process, revisions to the budget request are to be expected. Similar procedures are followed to acquire financial resources for nutrition activities in other government sectors and agencies.[2] Moreover, the budget office of the Ministry of Finance and Economic Planning refers to sectoral policies and the GPRS as the master development plan of government, both to establish reasonable budget ceilings for a sector and assess proposed

---

[2]An alternative mechanism for acquiring funding for public nutrition is through the district assemblies. However, this mechanism so far has not proved viable. Districts generally are unable to raise sufficient revenue on their own. Although the central government has ceded to the districts a broad range of sources of government revenue, Appiah et al. (2000, 90ff) show that between 65 and 90 percent of the revenue received by local governments continues to come from the central government. Moreover, much of the money that assemblies receive from the central government explicitly for district development purposes—a constitutionally mandated 5 percent of government revenue—is already earmarked for specific sectors or projects, and the assemblies have little discretion over its use.

However, even if financing from the District Assembly was available for nutrition activities, given a general lack of technical understanding of the actions needed to reduce undernutrition, convincing district policymakers of the wisdom of allocating the scarce financial resources they control to nutrition would be particularly challenging.

budget allocations within a sector. Policy statements are a key tool used in the annual government budget cycle.

With no policy on nutrition in place in Ghana, the bureaucratic process does little to allocate government financial resources in a way that ensures sufficient funding for the Nutrition Unit of the Ghana Health Service or other units involved with nutrition. There are considerable incentives for looking outside that process to acquire needed resources. Consequently, in the case of the Nutrition Unit, between two-thirds and three-quarters of its nonrecurrent funding for undertaking development programs is from external donors. However, even this level of government funding for nonrecurrent expenditures in nutrition is the highest of the four study countries.

Nutrition in National Policymaking Processes in Ghana

In this section, I examine in more detail prioritization at the national level concerning nutrition in Ghana. The key policymaking structures and actors, the narratives, and circumstances that might bring about a positive shift in the priority given to addressing undernutrition in Ghana are identified. A similar structure of presentation is used later in this chapter to describe the policy processes relating to nutrition in the other three study countries.

Structures.   The government of Ghana expends considerable effort in formulating policy to guide its action. Indeed, one respondent felt that "in Ghana, planning is done to the extreme, but we do not do such a good job at implementation." The policymaking structures are well defined and situated in the sectoral organization of government. Overall policy direction is the responsibility of the Council of Ministers. The National Development Planning Commission and the Ministry of Finance and Economic Planning coordinate the actual policy formulation and the allocation of resources for programming under the policies, respectively.

The sectoral ministries are responsible for the technical design and implementation of these programs.

In the case of nutrition, there are no national institutions outside the executive branch of government that are engaged in nutrition policy formulation. On nutrition issues, the parliament is not proactive but simply responds to submissions of various sorts from the sectoral ministries. It does not appear to hold the executive branch accountable for the nutrition status of the population. Neither of the two main political parties, the ruling New Patriotic Party or the National Democratic Party, made any mention of undernutrition as a policy problem in their platforms for the 2004 elections. Moreover, no civil institutions have emerged to energize policy processes on nutrition issues.

International donors and technical agencies working in Ghana in cooperation with the government are involved in nutrition policy, particularly in ensuring that nutrition programs are implemented. As mentioned earlier, UNICEF, the World Health Organization, and USAID, in particular, are involved in providing financial and technical support for nutrition programming of various sorts. However, these international agencies are not directly engaged in national policy processes. Rather, they provide national counterparts with a technical understanding of issues related to undernutrition that may require policy decisions to address effectively. Moreover, there is no formal coordination among these international agencies to determine jointly how they should work strategically with their Ghanaian counterparts on nutrition issues.

Actors.   At the time of the institutional study in 2004, nutrition issues were absent from the most prominent national-level policy process. Undernutrition was not singled out as a development problem that should be a main concern of government. Nutrition activities were being carried by the health sector and, in a more limited manner, by the agriculture and education sectors. No sense of urgency was attached to undernutrition. Existing public-sector mechanisms for addressing the issues were generally judged adequate. Consequently, the primary actors in the policy process in nutrition in Ghana are those responsible for the implementation of programs in nutrition—the head of the Nutrition Unit of the Ghana Health Service, most notably, but also the head of the women's program in the agriculture sector and the various nutritionists working on donor-supported nutrition programs. Less centrally, nutrition professors at University of Ghana and elsewhere could constitute important actors for energizing policy processes on undernutrition.

Formal coordination and advocacy groups for nutrition are poorly developed in Ghana. The only formal nutrition strategy for Ghana, the Ghana National Plan of Action on Food and Nutrition, proposed that a coordination group be established for nutrition at the National Development Planning Commission, which is mandated by law to convene and manage such groups. However, such a group was never established. Similarly, outside government, there are only a handful of efforts aimed at bringing nutrition-focused institutions and individuals together. The TANA project country team was one such group. Another, the Food and Nutrition Security Network of Ghana at the University of Development Studies in Tamale, seeks to build political commitment to reducing undernutrition. However, most respondents felt that its role in advocating for increased resources for combating malnutrition has not been realized, as it is based outside of Accra, groups together individuals primarily working at the district-level, and does not include national policymakers.

No policy champions for nutrition were active at the time of the study. The minister of Food and Agriculture at the time regularly expressed concern about the burden that undernutrition poses for Ghana, and the director-general of the Ghana Health Service had been supportive of nutrition activi-

ties and raising the general awareness of the different forms of malnutrition and how they can be combated. However, none of the interviewees for the study identified any highly placed individuals in the public sector as being persistent advocates for increasing the attention and resources government gives to the problem of undernutrition in Ghana. Policy processes on nutrition tend to be focused on implementation and dominated by mid-level technical bureaucrats who, although competent, are poorly positioned to bring substantive change in the priority accorded to the problem of undernutrition.

Narratives.   As is common in many countries in Africa since the late 1990s, poverty reduction has been the principal orientation of any new policies in Ghana, both those formulated to provide a master development framework for the country as a whole and those to guide sectorally specific action. The GPRS was formally accepted in early 2003 as the basis for Ghana's participation in the highly indebted poor countries (HIPC) debt relief initiative of the World Bank and the International Monetary Fund (GOG 2003). More importantly, the GPRS serves as the master development plan for the government of Ghana. The strategy is organized around five pillars: ensuring macroeconomic stability; increasing economic production and generating gainful employment through private-sector-led agro-based industry; human resource development and the provision of basic services; protecting the vulnerable; and governance and public-sector reform.

Given the discussion in Chapter 3 on nutrition as a public policy concern, there are openings in the GPRS for nutrition under the three pillars of increasing economic production and generating gainful employment, human resource development, and protecting the vulnerable. Improving nutritional status as a component of poverty reduction is addressed in the introductory overview sections of the GPRS. However, considerably less attention is given to improving nutrition in the action plans that follow. Undernutrition is seen to be an important aspect of poverty, but direct action to address the problem seemingly is not similarly viewed as an important poverty-reduction strategy. One of the National Development Planning Commission managers of the GPRS drafting process suggested that the lack of real participation by advocates for nutrition in the consultations on the content of the strategy meant that nutrition was virtually ignored as actions to implement it were planned. The GPRS development exercise between 2000 and 2002 appears to have been a missed opportunity for nutrition advocates to insert undernutrition and action to combat it as key elements in the dominant policy narrative of poverty reduction in Ghana.

At the level of sectoral policies in Ghana, undernutrition is compartmentalized as a health issue. The Ministry of Health and the Ghana Health Service ensure that nutrition activities fit within the scope of their policies and work plans. However, the rationale for doing so appears to be based on a more restricted understanding of the determinants of nutritional status than that presented in the conceptual framework for this report. Similarly, those goods and services necessary to achieve nutrition that are provided by other sectors of government are not considered in the limited discussions on nutrition in the policy documents of the health sector. Moreover, the broader contributions that improved nutrition can make to human and economic development in Ghana are not invoked to justify the nutrition actions of the health sector or any increase in allocations of government resources to those ends.

Similarly in agriculture, the sectoral plan, the Food and Agriculture Sector Development Policy was developed within the context of the GPRS and lays out a broad framework to guide the development of the agriculture sector in Ghana (MOFA 2002). However, in neither this policy nor the strategic plan (which provides detailed prescriptions for program and project develop-

ment) is direct mention made of how agriculture might contribute to the nutrition security, as opposed to the food security, of Ghana. Little attention is paid to how the nutrition activities of WIAD in the Ministry of Food and Agriculture will be supported in the Food and Agriculture Sector Development Policy; how such activities will contribute to the attainment of the policy objectives; or how agriculture, by contributing to improved nutrition through food security, dietary diversity, and increased income and consumption, aids Ghana's human and economic development.

Overall, in spite of the continued daunting levels of child undernutrition across Ghana and the salience of improved nutrition for economic growth and poverty reduction, advocates for increased attention to the problem of undernutrition in the country so far have not formulated or publicized a policy storyline that links the two issues. The dominant policymaking narrative of poverty reduction in Ghana should be extended and should identify undernutrition as one of the most significant barriers to achieving comprehensive poverty reduction. Then the multisectoral action needed to overcome it could be specified in the GPRS and related policies.

Circumstances for Policy Change on Nutrition. Undernutrition in Ghana is not perceived by the policy elites as an issue of urgency to which the government must respond if it is to retain its legitimacy. If it were, the 6 percent increase in the prevalence of stunting among children younger than 3 between 1998 and 2003 to almost 27 percent should have led to a detectable policy response. Rather, undernutrition is an issue that is generally considered to be a problem that government and, in particular, the health sector works on as best it can. Grindle and Thomas (1991, 83ff.) posit that any policy processes on issues characterized as business-as-usual tend to focus on bureaucratic arrangements, involve mid-level managers rather than political leaders, and provide much less impetus for deep-seated policy reform. This situation holds for Ghana. Consequently, there are few circumstances under which important change is possible in the priorities of the Ghanaian government concerning the problem of undernutrition.

The regular revision of the GPRS is the only planned event that may provide an important opportunity to change the manner in which undernutrition is viewed in policy processes. It is to be regularly updated through participatory consultations. This review provides an opportunity for advocates for increased public resources and attention to address undernutrition to ensure that undernutrition is included in the revised GPRS as a key objective in the attainment of nutrition security.

However, doing so will require organization for advocacy. The current array of actors on policy processes in nutrition are dispersed and rather isolated within sectors. Any links between them tend to be informal with limited operational aims. The community of nutritionists working at the national level in Ghana is currently insufficiently organized to undertake a strategic advocacy program to raise the profile of undernutrition as a development problem requiring greater public attention. Similarly, they are unable to coordinate their activities across sectors to address comprehensively the multiple determinants of nutritional status to ensure nutrition security for all Ghanaian households. Although few would fault the individual efforts made to reduce undernutrition in the country, with closer attention to the dominant policy processes and an organized engagement in those processes, significant reductions in undernutrition should be possible, thereby triggering important gains in human and economic development in Ghana.

Mozambique

Nutrition in the Public Sector in Mozambique

The official "home" of nutrition in the Mozambican government is not contested, but the issue is not simple. The only institu-

tions in Mozambique where there is technical capacity in nutrition, however thin it may be, are the Ministry of Health, a local nutrition-focused NGO, and international development NGOs operating in the country. The official policy home for nutrition, in contrast, lies in the Ministry of Agriculture and Rural Development (MADER) in the Secretariado Técnico de Segurança Alimentar e Nutrição (SETSAN), the national food security and nutrition secretariat. At the time of the institutional study in late 2002, SETSAN and the Ministry of Agriculture had almost no technical capacity to plan and coordinate nutrition activities.

The Ministry of Agriculture was not a primary participant in the formulation of Mozambique's strategy on food security and nutrition. The Ministry of Planning and Finance and the Ministry of Health took the lead in the strategy formulation. Nevertheless, when the cabinet approved the policy in 1998, it directed that the secretariat responsible for coordinating the various sectoral activities at the national level, SETSAN, be housed in the Ministry of Agriculture. Although the Ministry of Agriculture is primarily responsible for the agricultural production aspects of food security, it has no expertise in nutrition. In consequence, arguably the most neglected aspect of the food security and nutrition strategy in its implementation under SETSAN has been its nutritional content, particularly with regard to the nonfood determinants of nutritional status—the provision of health services; the various components of a healthy environment, including clean water, sanitation, and adequate housing; and appropriate care for the nutritionally vulnerable.

The membership of SETSAN is multisectoral and includes the Ministry of Planning and Finance, Ministry of Health, Ministry of Agriculture, Ministry of Industry and Commerce, Ministry of Women and Social Action, and some international NGOs. SETSAN also has equivalent organizations in each province. Although it was to be reorganized following the fieldwork for this study, operationally, the national level

SETSAN is further divided into two working groups. The first focuses on national food security. Interviewees interested in this aspect of SETSAN expressed satisfaction with the effectiveness of the secretariat. The second focuses on food security and nutrition policies, planning, analysis, and monitoring. Although this subset of activities is arguably the reason for the existence of SETSAN, the consensus is that it has been problematic to carry out effectively. This is largely because of the difficulties of undertaking cross-sectoral activities in an institutional environment that is organized along sectoral lines, as well as the human capacity and leadership constraints in the Ministry of Agriculture on nutrition issues.

The role of SETSAN is one of coordination rather than financing and implementation. The provincial SETSANs develop annual action plans that are compilations of sectoral activities planned in the province by the government and NGOs that touch on food security and nutrition. The annual action plan for the national SETSAN is made up of the provincial action plans, to which is added a work plan for the national secretariat. However, neither the provincial nor the national SETSANs have budgets for the implementation of these activities. Each activity in these action plans is to be undertaken and funded through the specific sector in question, as these activities also appear in the provincial and national action plans for the sector. In general, the provincial SETSANs were seen by interviewees who had worked with them to be more effective at coordinating action across sectors and adding value to sectoral activities in the provinces. Partly because competition between sectors for increased allocations of resources is somewhat stronger in Maputo than it is in the provinces, the coordination function of the national SETSAN has not been as successful.

The primary location for technical nutritionists within government in Mozambique is the Nutrition Section of the Department of Community Medicine of the Ministry of Health. This section has been notably productive in providing nutritional support to primary health care efforts in nutrition—child growth monitoring and mother–child health clinics, as well as nutritional supplementation and clinical nutritional rehabilitation work. The section helps build the national capacity in nutrition by training nutrition technicians for posting to provinces and districts to back-stop nurses working in primary health clinics. At the time of the fieldwork, this program was in its initial stages, with only a handful of trained technicians in the field. All of these activities have been done through the efforts of fewer than a half-dozen Mozambican nutritionists with some expatriate technical assistance and quite reliable levels of donor funding. Indeed, this external funding has been sufficiently reliable that the Section receives very little core budgetary support for its programs from the annual budget of the Ministry of Health. However, the lack of budgetary support also reflects the low profile that the Nutrition Section has within the Ministry.

In spite of these accomplishments, at the time of the institutional study fieldwork, the Nutrition Section was facing a staffing crisis. Several of the masters-level nutritionists had left to join NGOs or donor-funded projects. There were only two graduate nutritionists remaining in the Section. As there is no tertiary-level training in nutrition in Mozambique, training to maintain higher levels of nutrition expertise must be done abroad at considerable cost.

Nutrition activities are not found elsewhere in government. However, much more so than in the other study countries, NGOs implement most of the nutrition-related activities in Mozambique. At the time of the fieldwork, due to insufficient capacity in government agencies, much of the provision of social services in agriculture, health, and rural development at district and community levels was provided by international NGOs working in coordination with government. Those NGOs that received support from USAID primarily received it through

Title II development assistance in the form of food aid, either in-kind or monetized. Because of the funding source, nutrition has been an explicit component of the project design for these NGOs, and nutritional impact indicators are built into the monitoring and evaluation of the projects. Several projects funded by other donors than USAID also have nutrition components. These include a Food and Agriculture Organization of the United Nations nutrition project in Manica province, work on micronutrient supplementation by Helen Keller International, and work related to the increased consumption of vitamin A–rich foods, most notably orange-fleshed sweet potato in Zambezia province.

In terms of policy to guide action to reduce undernutrition, and the allocation of financial, material, and human resources for such action, the government of Mozambique has had in place since 1998 the Estratégia de Segurança Alimentar e Nutrição, the national food security and nutrition strategy noted earlier. The impetus for the strategy came through Mozambique's participation in international conferences on nutrition and food. The global objective of the strategy is to guarantee that all citizens have at all times physical and economic access to necessary food in a manner that will allow all to live an active and healthy life; it is primarily oriented toward food security rather than nutrition. Nutritional considerations are raised in the strategy to ensure that all individuals are able to utilize the food available to them in a manner that satisfies their nutritional needs. Moreover, it specifically acknowledges the strongly gendered roles that are played in households in guaranteeing food security and improving nutrition. The strategy does not lay out specific targets for the sectors involved. Rather, it sets priority activities for each under the three dimensions of food availability, access to food, and food utilization. It leaves specific sectoral mechanisms and objectives to be set by the ministries concerned.

The national food security and nutrition strategy fits under a hierarchy of other policy statements that are less definitive on the importance of improved nutrition for human and economic development. The master development plan for the government is the Plano de Acção para a Redução da Pobreza Absoluta (PARPA), the Action Plan for the Reduction of Absolute Poverty (Republic of Mozambique 2001), that also serves as the PRSP for Mozambique under the HIPC debt relief initiative. PARPA defines poverty as the "inability of individuals to ensure for themselves and their dependents a set of basic minimum conditions necessary for their subsistence and well-being in accordance with the norms of society" (Republic of Mozambique 2001, 11). Undernutrition is certainly an element of poverty, but the PARPA does not discuss in detail how the poverty reduction strategy will ensure that levels of undernutrition are reduced across Mozambique.

However, in terms of the allocation of government resources, any priority accorded to nutrition activities in government policy statements is not reflected strongly in the level of resources provided by government. As noted, virtually all of the operational expenses of the Nutrition Section of the Ministry of Health are provided by international donors, with one interviewee noting that because it has been very successful in getting donor funds, the Ministry almost expects it to get by without any core funding out of the allocation from central government. For SETSAN, no budget is provided directly to the secretariat by the government. Rather, resources are drawn from the annual budget allocation made to the Ministry of Agriculture. However, the Ministry is unwilling to cover the full costs of running the secretariat, as, in its view, SETSAN was established to coordinate intersectoral activities on food security and nutrition. Consequently, it feels that SETSAN should receive support from all participating sectors, with the result that the secretariat is left to operate with inadequate resources.

Nutrition in National Policymaking Processes in Mozambique

Structures. Over the past 15 years, the Mozambican government has engaged in considerable efforts at policymaking to bring the activities of a range of government sectors and subsectors in line with the market-oriented economic framework established for national development and with the overall government aim of poverty reduction through rapid and broad-based economic growth. As for all of the study countries, the policymaking structures of the government of Mozambique are situated principally in the executive branch. The body responsible for approving government policy is the Council of Ministers. The actual formulation of broad, multisectoral policies is coordinated principally by the Ministry of Planning and Finance, whereas sectoral policies and strategies are developed by the sectoral ministries concerned.

In considering the institutional structures involved in policy processes related to nutrition, the national food security and nutrition strategy was developed over several years in the mid-1990s under the leadership of the Ministry of Planning and Finance, with key support from the Nutrition Section of the Ministry of Health. As the strategy was considered cross-sectoral in scope from the outset of its development, other ministries were also involved in its formulation. Several interviewees noted that the initiative of the Nutrition Section in this policy process was to a large degree independent of the Ministry of Health as a whole.

Few other institutions are significant for policymaking on nutrition at the national level in Mozambique. The National Assembly and the two major political parties, FRELIMO and RENAMO, have not examined undernutrition with sufficient focus to result in any changes in the level of effort made to address the problem. Civil organizations with an interest in nutrition issues are absent. Moreover, international development partners for Mozambique seem to be somewhat less engaged in nutrition issues than is seen in other countries. Given that the country has spent the past 15 years pulling itself up from years of decline, this attitude may reflect the perception of a different set of development priorities facing Mozambique relative to the other three study countries. Although one should not minimize the important contributions to improved nutrition made by international NGOs working in the country, within the domain of nutrition policy formulation, the activities of international agencies are less noticeable.

Actors. At the time of the institutional study in Mozambique, the profile of nutrition in policy processes seemed to be in a state of decline. All interviewees viewed the official approval of the national food security and nutrition strategy in late 1998 as a success in establishing a foundation for substantially reducing undernutrition in Mozambique, even though it had occurred almost 4 years before. Several individuals were mentioned as key participants in that process—a director in the Ministry of Planning and Finance and the chief nutritionist and an expatriate nutrition advisor in the Nutrition Division of the Ministry of Health, most notably.

However, since that success, key actors in addressing undernutrition as a government priority in Mozambique are less obvious. As noted, the Nutrition Division itself had lost much of its expertise since the policy was passed, rendering it possibly less effective in implementing nutrition programming and certainly less effective in engaging in priority setting and resource allocation decisions to ensure that combating undernutrition remains a focus of government. SETSAN was established under the national food security and nutrition strategy and was functioning in the Ministry of Agriculture. At the time of the fieldwork, however, its leadership seemingly had little vision of how nutrition should feature in the suite of activities it coordinated, in part because of lack of familiarity with undernutrition as a public policy problem and lack of resources to address the issue.

Although the human capacity for nutrition programming in Mozambique is much less than in the three other study countries and is dangerously low, its level likely has increased in recent years, particularly with the program of training district-level nutrition technicians in the health sector and the continuing nutrition-oriented work of many NGOs. However, the presence of effective, key actors in nutrition policy processes at the national level has certainly declined. Those who were policy champions for nutrition earlier have moved on in their careers and are no longer affiliated with key institutions of the policy process. Although these former policy leaders can continue to speak out on nutrition issues, because they are now outside of government they are unlikely to foster change in government priorities and resource allocations. This is particularly the case when bureaucratic, rather than technical, issues dominate policy debates related to nutrition—such as how SETSAN might be restructured so that it is effective in its nutrition coordination role. As a consequence, without new nutrition advocates participating in national priority setting and resource allocation processes, it appears unlikely that the national government will increase its attention to the problem of undernutrition in Mozambique.

Narratives. The dominant framing of the problem of undernutrition in Mozambique is in the context of food security. The formal statement on national priorities related to nutrition is presented in the food security and nutrition strategy, in which food security is disaggregated into availability, access, and utilization of food. Nutrition concerns emerge in the strategy when considering the utilization of food. The implicit framework underlying this policy characterizes nutrition security as a subset of food security. That SETSAN is located in the Ministry of Agriculture follows from this understanding

of the problems of food security and nutrition, because, if the problem is food, the principal sector responsible for food in Mozambique should be responsible. In the narrative used in this report, in contrast, food security is identified as a component of nutrition security (see Figures 3.1 and 3.2).

The food-centered arguments of the 1990s were primarily justified by the continuing food insecurity in the country consequent to the civil war and recurrent natural disasters. Although Mozambique remains the most food insecure of the four study countries, positive trends have been seen for several years. As Shrimpton (2002, 21) notes in a draft strategy for the Nutrition Section, in Mozambique "food security should become less of an overriding national priority" and the notion that undernutrition will be solved just by "getting food into people" should increasingly be challenged. "Other substantive areas outside of food and/or nutrients are also important." Policy narratives both define the problem and suggest what action is required to tackle it. The food-security framework within which nutrition has been situated in policy discussions to date provides insufficient guidance on the determinants of nutritional status. Invoking a broad, nutrition-focused framework would considerably clarify what sort of actions are needed across various sectors to ensure that all Mozambicans enjoy nutrition security, rather than merely food security, and how they should be implemented and coordinated. Doing so would also enable a closer consideration than has so far been the case of those constraints on attaining broad, sustained improvements in nutritional status that are linked to gender disparities in access to resources.

Circumstances for Policy Change on Nutrition. As in Ghana, undernutrition is not an issue that threatens the legitimacy of the Mozambican government or that of the sectors concerned. With the formulation of a national policy on nutrition, that any subsequent policy implementation and modification has primarily focused on bureaucratic arrangements is unsurprising, given an understandable lack of urgency on the issue. As in the other study countries, prevalent chronic undernutrition is simply part of the broader complex of issues associated with underdevelopment in Mozambique but is seemingly not a target in its own right for public action in the short to medium term. As in Ghana, it is difficult to see how this situation might change considerably in the near future through the normal operation of the policy processes that are now in place in Mozambique.

However, two openings may bring incremental change in the attention given to undernutrition as a development problem for Mozambique. First, as in Ghana and Uganda, the Poverty Reduction Strategy process linked to the HIPC initiative requires that the strategy undergo regular participatory review and redrafting to reflect changing circumstances. In Mozambique, the PARPA was initially accepted in 2001, and a revision was completed in early 2006. If future assessments of this master development framework for the country enable broad participation, advocates for nutrition could engage in the discussions to ensure that improved nutrition be more central to the strategy.

Second, at the time of the fieldwork, SETSAN was not functioning to support nutrition programming in an effective way. Continuing dissatisfaction with SETSAN as a key element in the implementation of the national food security and nutrition strategy may eventually call into question the appropriateness of this policy to reduce undernutrition. Fostering such action may require a framing of the problem and its solutions in a manner that is distinct from the problem of food insecurity. A new, nutrition-specific policy may be required, with its own institutional arrangements to coordinate the implementation of its programs.

As it has emerged over the past 15 years from the devastation of civil war, Mozambique is a success story. However, under-

nutrition remains high, with little change over the past 10 years in the key indicators of the proportion of young children who are stunted or underweight. Without more attention to what the government should do to reduce undernutrition among its citizens, success in both human and economic development in Mozambique can be expected to lag. The current policies and institutional arrangements for public action against undernutrition are likely to be inadequate to remove the constraint undernutrition poses for enhanced development.

Nigeria

Nutrition in the Public Sector in Nigeria

In Nigeria, official responsibility for nutrition policy broadly considered lies with the National Planning Commission (NPC). A National Committee on Food and Nutrition (NCFN) was established in the NPC to develop the National Policy on Food and Nutrition (NPC 2001), coordinate nutrition activities across the sectors, and mobilize resources for nutrition. The NCFN brings together government ministries or agencies involved in nutrition-related activities, as well as academic experts in nutrition. The chair is the head of the Agriculture and Industry Department of the NPC. NPC was selected to have oversight on nutrition in recognition of the cross-sectoral nature of action necessary to improve nutrition. Moreover, given its central role in government planning and budgeting, it was hoped that the NPC would mobilize financial resources for nutrition activities.

Most respondents characterized the period just prior to when fieldwork was conducted as the high point of NPC's leadership in nutrition policy, having managed the development of the National Policy on Food and Nutrition from the time it was originally drafted in 1994 to its official adoption by the government in November 2002. This accomplishment was widely applauded.

Nevertheless, several problems were highlighted concerning NPC's role in coordinating nutrition activities. First, NPC has neither a comparative advantage nor any special expertise in nutrition. Consequently, its commitment to nutrition and to an effective NCFN is often felt to be wanting. The Commission is staffed by economists and planners. Only since the fieldwork was completed has a nutritionist been brought on staff at NPC to be responsible for the activities of the NCFN. Second, institutional memory on and commitment to nutrition issues is weak in NPC. There is rapid turnover in the Commission. For example, the chair of the NCFN who managed the official launch of the National Policy on Food and Nutrition was only in post for 4 or 5 months before being reassigned. Moreover, those civil servants selected to manage the NCFN typically bring with them no specialized nutritional understanding. Consequently, momentum on addressing nutrition issues and developing nutrition programming through the NPC is difficult to build and sustain. Finally, there are no signs that nutrition is privileged in the allocation of government resources by virtue of the presence of the secretariat of the NCFN in NPC. Indeed, the fact that virtually all costs for nutrition programming in Nigeria are borne by donors indicates that the NPC lacks necessary influence in this regard. However, when these criticisms of nutrition in the NPC were voiced, no interviewee suggested that the NCFN be placed elsewhere or that some other institution manage nutrition planning at the federal level.

The National Policy on Food and Nutrition mandates the establishment of counterpart institutions to the NCFN at the state and local levels "as appropriate and needed"

(NPC 2001, 22). These committees are to coordinate food and nutrition programs at those levels of government. Few of these state committees were operating effectively at the time of the fieldwork. In only a handful of the 774 Local Government Authorities in the country have committees been established, as, according to an agricultural officer from one in delta state, there is insufficient clarity on their composition, scope of work, or the resources they are to use to operate.

The NCFN is the official policy body on nutrition issues at the federal level. However, a parallel body, the Nutrition Partners group, was established in early 2002 as part of the effort that led to the formal adoption of the National Policy on Food and Nutrition by the Nigerian government. It has no official government standing, but brings into a common forum government agencies, donors, indigenous and international NGOs, the United Nations and other international organizations, and other organizations or individuals with an interest in nutrition. Although it includes members of the NCFN, it expands beyond the Committee considerably. This group allows for coordination among donors, between donors and their national partners in nutrition, and among nutritionists in Nigeria. To date, its focus has been on coordinating financial resources to support nutrition-related activities. The NPC is responsible for calling its meetings.

Technical activities in the public sector that are explicitly identified as being nutrition oriented are those related to primary health care.[3] The Nutrition Division in the Department of Community Development and Population Activities of the Federal Ministry of Health traditionally has had as

---

[3]In discussions with university professors in nutrition, the point was made that officially, nutrition in Nigeria has a strong medical tenor to it. Consequently, nutritionists trained or working in agricultural universities do not necessarily find a welcome place for their interests in the Nigerian nutrition community. As one professor of nutrition at an agricultural university noted, a vision of nutrition that is science-based, rather than medically-based, would allow for more productive cross-sectoral action on nutrition in Nigeria.

its primary function the formulation of appropriate national nutrition policy in the health sector, a function that is now subsumed in the larger cross-sectoral nutrition policy function of the NCFN. It also undertakes some technical implementation work in the field—nutrition surveillance in sentinel areas, training, national workshops on nutrition topics, child deworming efforts, goiter surveys, and so on. In the field, most of the work of the Division is done in collaboration with the National Primary Health Care Development Agency. The Nutrition Division is hampered by lack of funding and is generally dependent on donors for operational resources.

Most state ministries of health have comparable nutrition units responsible for coordinating all nutrition activities in the health sector of the state. As at the federal level, the state-level nutritionists interviewed complained of poor funding for carrying out their responsibilities. Very little support is obtained from the federal and state governments for nutrition programs, in part, these nutritionists claimed, because state politicians and policymakers are ignorant about the social benefits of improved nutrition, the determinants of nutritional status, and what public action is needed.

The National Primary Health Care Development Agency is the federal agency responsible for providing primary health care services. It is the principal institution responsible for seeing that nutritional deficiencies are directly addressed by health workers in communities across Nigeria. This work is done through programs in child growth monitoring, demonstrations of the preparation of locally adapted nutritious food and food preservation techniques, vitamin A and iron supplementation programs, and advocacy for exclusive breast-feeding. Moreover, all clients coming to Primary Health Care clinics are given a nutritional assessment. The agency is responsible for ensuring that clinic staff members are provided with the training and tools necessary to carry out these activities.

The degree to which nutrition-oriented activities feature in other sectors of government is small. Nutrition is not given much attention by the agricultural sector in Nigeria, with no nutritionists employed in the formal agricultural sector at federal and state levels. Although training in human nutrition is offered at agricultural universities, in the sector itself, food scientists and home economists are responsible for nutrition activities. The agriculture sector is primarily production oriented. A senior agricultural researcher noted that agriculturalists in Nigeria historically have been most concerned with raising yields and, second, with the profitability of farming. Agriculturalists might be willing to consider nutritional objectives, but at the end of the day, he asserted, increasing crop yields is the principal criterion used to judge the effectiveness of agriculturalists in Nigeria. The few policy and strategy documents for agriculture in Nigeria do not discuss how agriculture might serve to build the nutritional well-being of the population.

What nutrition activities there are in the agricultural sector are usually linked to women's programs that are run by home economists at federal and state levels. The technical work tends to focus on developing low-cost food preservation technologies and recipes for making use of locally available nutritious foods. The principal aim of the outreach and extension work of these women's programs is economic empowerment through developing off-farm income-generating activities. These community projects provide a means to disseminate nutrition messages as well as technologies that can contribute to improved nutrition in the household. However, a sustained, sufficient level of resources is not allocated to continuously run such programs.

Although nutrition has a low profile in the agricultural sector, it is more prominent in education. In the primary and secondary education system, nutrition is part of the home economics curriculum. Home economics is a core, compulsory subject in both primary and junior secondary school. In senior secondary, students can choose to study in three different areas of home economics, one of which is food and nutrition. National examinations are given in the subject area.

At university level, human nutrition is an important academic discipline. At least four universities award Ph.D.s in Human Nutrition or closely allied fields—Abeokuta, Ibadan, Nsukka, and Umudike. Nutrition training is offered in several other universities and polytechnics. With the relatively large number of tertiary-level training opportunities, there are sufficient numbers of professional nutritionists for posting to all state and federal nutrition positions.

Nigeria's considerable human capacity in nutrition is represented by the Nutrition Society of Nigeria. The Society leadership estimates that there are at least 500 professionally trained nutritionists in the country (masters level or above). The Society holds annual general meetings of a technical and professional nature. Its president is an institutional member of the NCFN. However, in general it has not been particularly vocal or effective in communicating to policymakers and the general public why undernutrition is an important policy problem for Nigeria and what should be done to address the problem. There was little evidence found in the study that the Society had positioned itself as an institutional source of objective information relating to nutrition in debates. Nigeria is unique among the study countries in having such a civil organization. With strategic engagement with the federal government, it could be an effective participant in nutrition policy processes, particularly in ensuring that policy is formulated based on a clear understanding of the evidence.

Outside the government, there are relatively few international organizations and NGOs working on public nutrition issues. The World Health Organization and UNICEF have been the longest international supporters of nutrition in Nigeria. Since 1999, USAID has also been active in nutrition, both

directly at the federal level working with the NCFN and at local levels through the Nigerian program of BASICS II for the integrated management of childhood illness. The International Institute for Tropical Agriculture, based in Ibadan, has also been involved in surveys on nutritional status. Smaller projects with nutrition components are implemented on local scales across the country by other NGOs, both national and international.

In terms of policy to guide action to reduce undernutrition and the allocation of financial, material, and human resources for such action, the National Policy on Food and Nutrition was officially launched by the government in 2002. The goal is to improve the nutritional status of all Nigerians, with particular attention to vulnerable groups. It implicitly draws on the conceptual framework of the determinants of nutritional status presented in Figure 3.2, with three specific objectives linked to the underlying determinants of that framework of improving food security, enhancing caregiving capacity, and improving the provision of human services (including health care, sanitation, and education). Two additional objectives of the policy are to improve capacity to address food and nutrition issues and to raise awareness and understanding of the problem of undernutrition in Nigeria. An action plan for implementing the National Policy on Food and Nutrition was published in 2003 (NPC 2003). This plan is organized within the framework of the five objectives of the policy, with specific goals and strategies established under each guiding the selection of specific activities. Each of these activities is assigned to lead agencies in government, and the costs of each are estimated. It is proposed that the action plan be implemented between 2004 and 2015 at an estimated cost over the 12 years of $250 million.

Turning to the funding of public nutrition programs, although the federal government, particularly in President Obasanjo's second term of office since 2003, has made progress in establishing a more transparent and policy-driven system for budgeting and resource allocation, it does not yet work efficiently. In 2004, the government published the NEEDS, its first master development policy (NPC 2004). Financial management has been tightened. The Ministry of Finance now requires that sectoral ministries develop medium-term sectoral strategies and submit annual budget requests that are justified by reference to government and sectoral policy and the medium-term strategies, although without much success. A key constraint on building a more rational resource allocation system at the federal level is a legacy of personal decisionmaking on how resources are allocated. To a large degree, this problem reflects the political complexity of the country. As a consequence, in most federal ministries planning is ineffectual, without generally agreed upon sets of priorities for each sector, and the weight accorded to technical inputs to policy debates is considerably less than in the other three study countries. Formal policy statements, at least at the sector level, are not used. The result is a lack of predictability and structure in the manner in which resources are allocated.

Although there is a formal set of priorities for nutrition activities established in the National Policy on Food and Nutrition and its action plan, these documents so far have done little to increase the allocation of federal resources to combating undernutrition. Among the reasons are that the sector-specific priorities laid out in the policy and its action plan are not included in budget requests of the sectors involved because of the lack of advocacy in those sectors. As a resource mobilization tool, the National Policy on Food and Nutrition and the action plan developed to implement it have not been very effective in increasing the allocation of resources by the federal government to nutrition activities. Government funding for nutrition activities has not changed substantially since the adoption of the policy.

Nutrition in National Policymaking Processes in Nigeria

Structures. The scale and complexity of Nigeria is considerably greater than that of the other three study countries. Nigeria is a heterogeneous, federal nation that has a complicated history of political conflict among social groups. Nigeria is much less stable politically, and the stakes involved in any change in the way government operates appear to be much higher than in the other three countries. Consequently, political considerations far outweigh technical ones in determining the extent to which undernutrition is treated as a policy problem at national level in Nigeria.

Although a democratic system of government has been in place since 1999, decisionmaking on government priorities and the allocation of resources still reflects the centralized autocratic regimes of previous decades in many respects. Such a system enables the regime in power to use government resources more flexibly to meet political demands from various quarters. As such, policymaking remains almost as personalized as it was under military rule. Since 1999, the president has relied on small groups of experts to formulate many of the sectoral and subsectoral policies and action plans his regime has instituted. These are often implemented as Presidential Initiatives rather than as an element of strategies defined by the sectoral ministries concerned. There is no debate either in the technical sectors involved or in national legislative bodies, such as the National Assembly, as to the merits of the plans as they are being formulated, and it is not clear what criteria are used to prioritize these initiatives. Improved nutrition has not featured directly among these initiatives.

Given this pattern of policymaking at the federal level, the nominal policymaking structures that should ensure that necessary nutrition-related goods and services are provided to undernourished Nigerians are ineffectual. These structures—principally the sectoral ministries that have responsibility for elements of the various determinants of nutritional status—are not involved in broad priority setting. Policy is dictated to them by the office of the president. The relatively poor policy environment at the sectoral level is both an outcome and a contributing factor to this situation. With experience showing that statements of policy are somewhat irrelevant to how resources are allocated to the sector, there are few incentives for sectors to establish formal sectoral policies. In the absence of such statements, the office of the president believes that it is justified in establishing the priorities for the sector by the allocation of funding and other resources to it. Consequently, policymakers in the office of the president—with even less knowledge than sectoral managers of the significance of undernutrition as a policy problem—are responsible for determining how undernutrition is addressed by the government. Because undernutrition is not a political issue that sparks conflict among political groups in Nigeria, it is generally ignored by the principal institutions involved with establishing policy at federal level. Because of this manner of making policy and allocating resources, the NCFN as a body responsible for coordinating nutrition policy in Nigeria is peripheral to the main policy thrusts of the federal government.

Actors. With the principal policymaking structure of significance at the national level being the office of the president, those actors in nutrition policy processes who may be particularly effective are linked somehow to the office of the president. The NPC is a part of the office of the president, as the head of NPC is the chief economic advisor to the president. The NPC also houses the secretariat for the NCFN and, as such, is officially responsible for federal nutrition policy. However, as noted earlier, the NPC has been relatively ineffective as a leader for nutrition in the broader policy and resource allocation processes to date. Coupled with a lack of capacity, there has been little sustained attention from the NPC leadership on how government should evaluate and address the issue of undernutrition. If the intellectual resources and standing of the membership of the NCFN are drawn on, the leadership of the NPC is well situated to advocate for increased attention to nutrition.

Particularly in a personalized policymaking environment, highly placed advocates who have access to political leaders can bring about significant changes in the priority given to nutrition. Several interviewees highlighted the important role that the late Dr. Olikoye Ransome-Kuti, a former federal minister of health who established the National Primary Health Care Development Agency, played in this regard in the 1980s and 1990s both for nutrition and primary health care in general. However, no champions for nutrition have emerged at the highest levels of government in Nigeria in recent years.

Considering implementation as an element of the nutrition policy process, the members of the Nutrition Partners group, both jointly and individually, are among the most significant actors. The group brings together technical practitioners, development partners of government, and key government ministries. Although the policy successes enjoyed by the group are primarily linked to the adoption of the national policy and the development of an action plan, the coordination achieved through the group and the donor resources mobilized for implementing programs provide a foundation for increased advocacy in the federal government that could lead to success in attracting attention to, and devoting increased government resources toward, combating undernutrition.

Narratives. Formal policy narratives are poorly developed at the national level in Nigeria. When the country was under military rule, there seemingly was little need for explicit policy statements that defined the principal challenges that government would address and how it would do so. This attitude is still prevalent across sectors at the federal level. It was only in 2004, well into the second term of the civilian Obasanjo administration, that the NEEDS document was published as the government's master development policy (NPC 2004). The objectives of this policy are wealth creation, employment generation, poverty reduction, and value reorientation. Although Nigeria is not part of the HIPC initiative of the World Bank and the International Monetary Fund, NEEDS contains many of the same elements as the PRSPs that HIPC countries have drafted to guide their own investments to reduce poverty, including those developed by the three other study countries.

Nutrition features in NEEDS only within the context of human rights, under which "the government recognizes the individual's rights and responsibilities and promises to deliver the basic necessities for a decent human existence" (NPC 2004, 28). Listed among these necessities is adequate nutrition. However, improved nutrition is not considered in the NEEDS as a strategic instrument for building the human capacity necessary to achieve the sustained wealth creation, employment generation, and poverty reduction sought under the strategy.

In contrast, the National Policy on Food and Nutrition has a more expansive view of the importance of good nutrition for Nigerian society as both a "pre-condition for development and a key objective of progress in human development" (NPC 2001, iii). However, there is little in NEEDS to indicate that the national policy was used to guide its content. Although NEEDS and the National Policy on Food and Nutrition do not stand in opposition, the more ambitious objectives of the policy are not necessarily endorsed by NEEDS, given the more limited view of the scope of nutrition as a policy problem in the master development policy.

Circumstances for Policy Change on Nutrition. Relative to the other three study countries, Nigeria is politically unstable. Consequently, during changes in national leadership, there is considerable scope for important modifications to the priority that the federal government accords efforts to reduce undernutrition. Past changes in national leadership have typically led to a broad reformulation of policy for the government as a whole and at the sector level. Reformulation of policy is an element in the reallocation of government resources to build support for a new administration from politically important groups. Even during democratic changes in leadership, as planned for 2007 when President Obasanjo will have met his term limit, this pattern is likely to be maintained. Important development objectives can be served during such periods when the agendas for policymaking are considerably more open than later, when the new administration has secured its power base. With strategic engagement by nutrition advocates during such periods, significantly increased attention could be paid to addressing undernutrition.

However, frequent policy change—on a 4- or 8-year cycle if current electoral arrangements are maintained—will as likely lead to a diminution in government's attention to undernutrition as to an increase. This possibility is particularly likely if key actors in nutrition policy, such as the NCFN and members of the Nutrition Partners group, are unable to participate in the processes through which a new regime establishes its policies. Moreover, even if support is maintained, changes in the content of the existing policies on nutrition or in the sectors critical to attaining sustained nutrition security will likely inhibit the attainment of medium to long-term objectives that require a predictable, long-term programmatic commitment. Although changes in national leadership do provide an opportunity for enhanced attention to nutrition as a policy problem, there is much to be said for new Nigerian political leaders judiciously respecting existing policies when they are being implemented effectively.

Beyond leadership change, international policy narratives also may affect the manner in which the Nigerian government addresses undernutrition. An important macroeconomic objective of the economic reforms sought by President Obasanjo was international debt forgiveness. This goal was achieved in 2005, with the Nigerian government committing itself to use the debt savings to tackle poverty. This poverty reduction effort has been placed in the framework of both the NEEDS and the Millennium Development Goals (MDGs). Programming the significant resources that Nigeria will now have available from the cancellation of its international debt to attain the MDGs could bring about a change in the way the government prioritizes its efforts to reduce undernutrition. Reducing undernutrition is a key element in attaining the first MDG to eradicate extreme poverty and hunger (World Bank 2006a, 34ff.). If the target for the first MDG of reducing by half the prevalence of underweight preschoolers is to be achieved by 2015 in Nigeria, significantly more direct action in nutrition will be required.

Over the past eight years, the federal government of Nigeria has become more transparent in the allocation of the considerable resources under its control. Attempts to put in place some formal policy-making mechanisms are part of this effort, as is improved macroeconomic management and government budget proesses. However, it is unclear whether these changes will be sustained by new leaders. The lack of effective engagement by actors for nutrition in national policy processes may be understandable, given that these processes remain considerably disordered and unpredictable. Successes within the limited context of the National Policy on Food and Nutrition are worth highlighting. However, the human and economic costs associated with the high level of undernutrition in the country do require considerably greater effort. This high level

is evidence that so far, the sectors at federal government level responsible for addressing undernutrition generally have failed in meeting their responsibilities in this regard.

Uganda

Nutrition in the Public Sector in Uganda

The Uganda Food and Nutrition Council (UFNC) was established by the government in 1964 shortly after independence. It had a fitful and often contentious existence over the next 35 years. The institutional placement of the secretariat for the Council as the official location for nutrition policy oversight in the Ugandan government was a regular point of conflict between the agriculture and health sectors during that period. However, beginning in 2002 (shortly before the institutional study fieldwork), the Plan for the Modernisation of Agriculture (PMA) secretariat led a concerted effort aimed at achieving the adoption by government of the Uganda Food and Nutrition Policy. The PMA secretariat also took responsibility for providing secretariat services for the UFNC. The PMA is the principal economic development strategy emerging from the Poverty Eradication Action Plan (PEAP), the master development framework for the government of Uganda (MFPED 2000). Although focused on agriculture, the plan has been promoted as multisectoral in scope, concerned with both economic and rural development, but with recognition of the need to focus on agriculture as the engine of growth for the Ugandan economy. The implementation of the plan is managed by a multisectoral steering committee chaired by the Ministry of Finance, Planning, and Economic Development, in which the secretariat for the PMA is housed.

Under the leadership of the PMA secretariat, the UFNC was successful in obtaining cabinet approval for the policy and, subsequently, developed a strategy for its implementation (MAAIF and MOH 2003, 2005). The Uganda Food and Nutrition Policy highlights the multisectoral dimensions of actions to promote food and nutrition security at all levels in the country. Consequently, multisectoral coordination is required for its implementation. The policy affirms that the UFNC will be responsible for performing this task. Although the policy does not mandate the PMA secretariat to host the UFNC, the cross-sectoral orientation of the PMA secretariat and the Ministry of Finance is in keeping with the multisectoral orientation of the Uganda Food and Nutrition Policy. However, contention remains on the issue of where the UFNC should be housed, as the strategy developed for the implementation of the policy specifically recommends that it be located in the Office of the Prime Minister, rather than in the PMA secretariat (MAAIF and MOH 2005, 25).

Decentralization of government functions and policy formulation are more advanced in Uganda than in the other study countries. The Uganda Food and Nutrition Policy stipulates that the implementation of the policy at district, subcounty, and community levels should be coordinated through existing multisectoral committees in the government bodies at those levels. However, the policy is vague on how these existing committees will develop the expertise on food and nutrition security necessary to analyze, plan, and promote coordinated activities across sectors to address nutritional problems at local levels.

Similarly, Uganda is the most advanced of the four study countries in building gender analysis into its policy and program planning and implementation processes and in articulating how a gender perspective provides important, useful insights. Nevertheless, there are no well-documented examples of how the application of gender analysis to nutrition programming in the country has led to significant improvements in broad nutritional status.

Technical activities in nutrition in the public sector are primarily located in the health and agriculture sectors. The Ministry of Health has a strong tradition of clinical nutrition centered on the rehabilitation of the severely malnourished. The Nutrition Section in the Child Health Division of the Department of Community Health, staffed by several masters-level nutritionists, centers its attention on primary health and integrated child health care packages provided by clinics across the country. However, interviewees stated that nutrition issues fall far down the list of priorities in the work undertaken by community-level health workers.

The agriculture sector has been involved with nutrition from at least 1964, when the Ministry of Agriculture was given responsibility for leading the UFNC. Although recent Ministers of Agriculture have been strong advocates for raising the profile of nutrition in agricultural policies and programs in Uganda, the ministry itself has quite limited human resources in nutrition. In recent years, there have been cutbacks in the resources allocated to nutrition work in the ministry. The principal location for technical nutrition work in the Ministry of Agriculture, Animal Industry and Fisheries, is in the Home Economics and Nutrition Unit. Until the 1980s, it was responsible for much of the home economics content of the national agricultural extension service. However, as was also seen in Ghana, thereafter home economics largely dropped out of extension, with a change in extension methodology. Following additional restructuring consequent to government decentralization, the start of the implementation of the PMA, and the formation of a new extension system, the Unit is now understaffed and has few government resources to implement programs.

Training in human nutrition at higher levels of education has received surprisingly little attention in Uganda. Although diploma courses in home economics have been available for many years and degree programs exist in food science, it has only been since 2003 that Uganda has had any degree programs focused on human nutrition. Previously, Ugandans seeking higher training in nutrition would go abroad. Not only did the lack of training limit understanding of the nutritional condition of the Ugandan population, it also proved to be an important constraint on effectively implementing nutrition programs. At the primary and secondary levels, a food and nutrition syllabus is followed in senior secondary schools, while the health syllabus in primary school includes nutrition.

Finally, in the public sector at the national level, several respondents highlighted the potential role for the multipurpose community development workers as an important avenue for building nutritional knowledge in the rural areas and, potentially, of building local demand for nutrition interventions. In the past, these workers were typically trained in home economics and were responsible for providing instruction on a range of issues to community members and for mobilizing the community to handle local development needs. Nutrition and food issues were an important part of their extension message. However, the institutional arrangements under which they worked and their roles have changed in recent years. The community development workers are staff of the Ministry of Gender, Labour, and Social Development, which has a small budget. They receive few resources to conduct their own programs. In many cases, they only work to support local projects that are funded by donors or another ministry. Moreover, the job description for the community development workers has changed. Social work and social protection activities—adult literacy, child rights, community mobilization, and the like—are now more typical of their tasks. Nutrition is almost wholly absent from the content of their job.

Outside the public sector, several international development NGOs work in Uganda and undertake nutrition activities as part of their relief work in northern Uganda and broader development work elsewhere. Moreover, there are smaller Uganda-based NGOs engaged in action-research projects that have nutrition as a component, such as the Regional Center for Quality of Health Care, which is working on disseminating vitamin-A rich orange-fleshed sweet potato. A nutrition advocacy NGO, the Uganda Action for Nutrition, was formed several years ago, but, so far has not established a place for itself in discussions on nutrition policy.

In terms of policy to guide the allocation of financial, material, and human resources for public action to reduce undernutrition, the use of all government resources are expected to be compliant with the PEAP, as the master development framework for Uganda, and with the PMA, the principal economic development strategy emerging from the PEAP. The Uganda Food and Nutrition Policy is consistent with both of these policies, but, so far, the acceptance of the policy by the government in 2003 does not seem to have changed allocations of government resources to nutrition activities. The strategy for implementing the policy was completed in 2005, but it is as yet unclear what effect it will have on the level of effort by the government to combat undernutrition. This strategy establishes a set of priority activities in 10 areas, particularly focusing on addressing the needs of nutritionally vulnerable groups. For each of the activities, a lead role is assigned to a specific public agency, with other agencies designated as collaborating partners in the effort. Finally, the plan suggests a generalized sequencing for when the actions should be undertaken. However, the action plan does not establish any costs for carrying out the actions, as these are to be determined during the additional planning required for their implementation.

Nutrition is not particularly prominent in any sectoral policy documents. The levels and trends in funding for nutrition activities within sectors reflect this neglect. In the agriculture sector, funding for nutrition activities have clearly declined over the past 15 years. In the health sector, resources for nutrition activities appear to be provided on a routine basis, with no scope for significant new attention in the sector to the problem of undernutrition. Because the Ministry of Finance also coordinates the annual budget process, the positioning of the UFNC in the PMA secretariat in the Ministry of Finance may lead to increased funding for nutrition. However, the mechanisms by which this increase would occur are not clear, and there is no evidence so far that funding for nutrition activities has increased since the PMA secretariat has coordinated the UFNC.

Finally, international donor funding is an important resource for the Ugandan government in carrying out its activities—typically more than 40 percent of the annual budget is funded by donors. However, despite this level of funding, international organizations and donors have somewhat less leverage in policy debates and program implementation than is commonly seen in Sub-Saharan Africa. An important reason is that many of Uganda's development partners have agreed to provide their support through basket funding, where all funds go to the government, and the government distributes the funds according to its own priorities without donor involvement. This development is desirable, as it reflects donor confidence in the abilities of the government of Uganda to allocate resources appropriately to meet its development objectives. However, in consequence, the degree to which large-scale action to address undernutrition is undertaken in Uganda will be dependent primarily on the government's inclusion of undernutrition among its development priorities. As seen, for example, in the case of USAID providing significant support to nutrition activities in Ghana, in Uganda the particular preferences of individual donors for action that focuses on the undernourished can be expected to be less

significant in influencing whether such action is taken.

Nutrition in National Policymaking Processes in Uganda

Structures. Concentrated efforts at formulating explicit sectoral policies and cross-sectoral economic development plans have been an important characteristic of the Ugandan state for the past 15 years. Given the relatively small size of Uganda and the desire of Ugandans—emerging in the late 1980s from two decades of political and socioeconomic instability—to work in a broad-based, coordinated fashion toward higher standards of living, Museveni and his allies have been able to impose what is essentially a benevolent autocracy, at least at the national level. Uganda's leaders privilege ambitious policy solutions that are supported by technical analysis, and their implementation is not overly constrained by the political negotiation and compromise necessary in a much larger and politically more complex state, such as Nigeria.

The principal structures involved in policymaking are centered on the office of the president and the administrative and sectoral agencies of government, which both formulate policy proposals for and implement the decisions made by the office of the president. The lead government agency for policy reform has been the Ministry of Finance, primarily because of its central role in master development planning, the acquisition and allocation of resources, and monitoring and evaluation of sectoral programs and policy initiatives. The sectoral agencies are responsible for the technical content of government policy and programs and are involved in sectoral policy formulation and program design. However, in performing this function, they are subject to the relatively strong oversight of the office of the president and the Ministry of Finance.

The National Assembly is the legislative branch of the government of Uganda, but it does not take a lead in policymaking. Although policies and institutional arrangements need to be approved by the Assembly, it rarely acts independently of the office of the president on these issues. It was not involved in the process through which the Food and Nutrition Policy was formulated, for example.

Of potential significance for the development of policy in nutrition is the emerging decentralized system of government in Uganda. This system incorporates a bottom-up planning process in which the concerns expressed through the village council are fed into the planning process up the hierarchy of local governments to the district level. At two points in this process, technical inputs are possible. At the subcounty and district levels, local government sectoral specialists—in health, education, agriculture, and so on—are part of the planning process and are able to advise and sensitize the councilors on issues of importance in their sectors.

However, the decentralized, bottom-up policy process that is desired for Uganda remains weak. Study informants generally agreed that most planning in Uganda is still top-down. Local revenue collection is poor, so local government councils have few resources that are directly under their control. Ninety percent of local government revenue is from the central government, with most of it provided in the form of conditional grants. As conditional grants are made to support national sectoral priorities and programs in the local government areas, they primarily reflect central government priorities.

Finally, international donors have constituted an important feature of the policy landscape in Uganda during the past 15 years. Their continuing importance as a source of government funding was noted earlier. Donors have also supplied considerable technical assistance to the government of Uganda as it formulated its development policies and programs. However, in recent years, the government of Uganda has asserted greater independence from these donors. This independence is seen in the political arena, where Museveni has rejected key elements of the political reforms expected by donors—most notably in 2005 by successfully removing constitutional limits on his term as president of the country. More constructively, because the government has established a track record of transparent and effective use of past donor support, several important donors now allow the government of Uganda full control on how the funds they provide will be used. Consequently, the profile of donors in policy processes, although still important, is less so than it was.

Actors. Nutrition has not been placed high on the agendas of those closely engaged in national policy processes in Uganda. Recent action to complete the long development of the Uganda Food and Nutrition Policy and subsequently develop a strategy for the policy is as much a result of events that brought attention to issues of food security and nutrition in national debates in Uganda as from the efforts of any actors in the policy process. What impetus to these efforts that has come from individuals is primarily from those in the agriculture sector. Several interviewees mentioned the leadership role in nutrition played in the early 1990s by the then Minister of Agriculture, Victoria Sekitoleko. Her successor some 10 years later, Wilberforce Kisamba-Mugerwa, also is given credit for re-energizing the Food and Nutrition Policy development process.

However, guiding the specific efforts involved in finalizing the policy and then developing the strategy were key administrators in the secretariat for the PMA. These individuals did not have any particular expertise in either food security or nutrition. But the secretariat had the necessary resources, human capacity, and political weight to manage and complete the task. The PMA secretariat staff members were able to mobilize a cross-sectoral steering committee to build broad commitment to the process, which enabled the policy to be approved and the strategy to be developed.

In examining the actors in nutrition policy processes in Uganda during fieldwork, of note was the lack of engagement by nutritionists in the broad policy processes of the country. The Uganda's poverty reduction strategy, the PEAP, and the PMA were the most prominent policy initiatives in Uganda at the time of the fieldwork. However, most of the nutritionists interviewed in Uganda did not recognize these policies as important for their own efforts to reduce undernutrition in the country. In interviews, they often were quite dismissive of these policies—particularly nutritionists in the health sector commenting on the relevance of the PMA to their work—or did not see any strategic value for nutrition programming in engaging in the discussions of such policies. Greater awareness of major policy debates and knowledge of how to engage in them seemed to be missing in most Ugandan nutrition experts. In this regard, Ugandan nutritionists were not very different from those in the other three study countries. Moreover, subsequent to the fieldwork, Ugandan nutritionists participated effectively in the revision of the PEAP in 2004, resulting in a broadening of the attention given to the problem of undernutrition in Uganda in this key policy.

Narratives.   Article 22 of the Preamble to the 1995 Constitution for Uganda commits the government to ensure that sufficient food is available for the citizens of the country and to encourage and promote proper nutrition. This statement is part of a set of articles titled the "Protection and Promotion of Fundamental and Other Human Rights and Freedoms." Under this constitution, the undernourished in Uganda are judged not to be enjoying their full rights as citizens of the country, and the government of Uganda has a duty to ensure their right to attain good nutritional status.

However, the master development framework for the country at the time of fieldwork, the 2000 version of the Poverty Eradication Action Plan, does not incorporate this understanding of the obligations of government concerning the nutritional status of the population, nor does it explicitly link undernutrition to poverty. In defining poverty, it focuses almost exclusively on income and consumption. This orientation of the policy caused unease among those interviewees whose own work focuses on elements of welfare other than raising incomes or consumption levels. To illustrate this tension, when interviewees were asked whether higher levels of income would solve problems related to undernutrition in Uganda, several independently noted that Bushenyi District in southwestern Uganda is among the least-poor districts in the country on income or consumption measures, yet it numbers among those districts with the highest prevalence of stunted children. As the PEAP was based on a limited concept of human welfare, these respondents felt that the PEAP likely would not directly reduce the level of undernutrition in Uganda.

Similarly, although the PMA adopts as one of its broad strategies the guaranteeing of food security through commercial agriculture, the concept of food security is not sufficiently well defined in the plan to assess how generally improved nutritional status will result. Moreover, no attention is paid to how the complementary underlying determinants of improved nutritional status —proper nutritional care, health services, and a hygienic environment—will be provided. Nutrition is given attention in two places in the PMA. First in discussing how the plan will be implemented across government ministries, the Ministry of Health is given responsibility "for nutrition and health services" under the PMA, without elaboration (MAAIF and MFPED 2000, 86). Second, the PMA calls for all programs falling within the scope of the PMA to be consistent with its aims, which include "contribution . . . to food security (and improved nutrition)" (MAAIF and MFPED 2000, 89). However, the PMA does not explicitly consider how its implementation will improve the nutritional status of Ugandans.

The Uganda Food and Nutrition Policy is the principal policy narrative on the problem of undernutrition and what should be done about it. In specifying the actions needed to ensure food and nutrition security, the policy is relatively comprehensive. However, no compelling storyline is developed in the policy to justify such a policy—that is, to define the problem that the policy will address and show how that problem links to the broader development aims of the government. Given the centrality of poverty reduction as a development objective of the government, it is odd that the interrelationship between improved nutritional status and economic growth is not made explicit in the Uganda Food and Nutrition Policy to make clear how it is aligned with the PEAP. Similarly, a conceptual framework of the determinants of nutritional status is not provided in the policy to guide the prioritization of public actions listed in the policy or to judge whether key interventions are missing. The rationale expressed in the policy for attention to the problem of undernutrition likely is not sufficient to compel any impartial policymaker at the national level to view its implementation as a priority.

Finally, in discussing narratives to foster policy change and attention to policy problems, nutrition is disadvantaged in the decentralized policymaking system emerging in Uganda because of a general lack of understanding both of the full scope of the economic and human burden of undernutrition and of what needs to be done to sustainably address it. There is considerable potential for decentralization to facilitate actions to improve nutritional status. One can assume that reducing hunger and improving the nutritional status of family members and neighbors would be a priority issue for vil-

lage councils. This concern would feed into the bottom-up policymaking system being established. However, for decentralization to work to improve nutrition, knowledge is needed. "How can you ask for things you don't know about?" was a frequent comment in interviews. A knowledge gap must be bridged at local levels if nutrition is to become a more significant part of the content of local government policy debate, planning, and action.

Circumstances for Policy Change on Nutrition. The manner in which policy changes in nutrition might come about in Uganda is similar to those operating in the other study countries. It was highlighted in the sections on Ghana and Mozambique that the regular PRSP revisions expected under the HIPC initiative provide an opportunity for engagement in these processes by nutrition advocates. This opportunity also holds for Uganda. The 2005 PEAP that was developed following the fieldwork for this study pays significantly more attention to undernutrition and the action to address it as a key element of human development (MFPED 2005). Ugandan nutrition advocates participated in the PEAP review process with success.

International policy dialogues also can be an important impetus for change. In April 2004, an international conference cosponsored by IFPRI, Assuring Food and Nutrition Security in Africa by 2020, was held in Uganda, with high-level participation from across the continent. It is noted in the strategy document for the implementation of the policy that the effort to formulate the strategy built upon the momentum fostered by this conference to insert food and nutrition security more centrally in government policy. The team writing the strategy was able to move the process much closer to completion as a consequence.

Finally, changes in the manner in which policy is formulated or changes in the participants in that process also provide an opportunity for increased attention to the problem of undernutrition in Uganda. Since 1995, the country's leadership has faced increasing challenges from those seeking broader participation in policymaking. If these pressures are sustained and the political system evolves in coming years, the resultant changes in the political landscape will provide possibilities that can be strategically exploited by advocates to increase the attention and resources given efforts to reduce undernutrition in Uganda.

Cross-Country Summary

Table 5.2 summarizes the results of this chapter using the four elements of the policy process that were considered for each study country. In this section, the significant similarities and differences among the four study countries are highlighted to motivate the suggestions made in the final chapter on additional actions that could enhance the profile of nutrition in national policy processes. There are more similarities than differences among the countries in the treatment of nutrition in their policy processes.

Similarities

Unfortunately, the dominant commonality is that undernutrition has not been prioritized effectively in any of the study countries. The presence of large numbers of undernourished in their populations has not resulted in concerted efforts by the governments to address the problem. The issue is certainly not dealt with in any of the four countries as a crisis requiring immediate action led by national leaders. Rather, what attention is given to undernutrition is through normal bureaucratic processes of the sectors that have been given or see themselves as having a mandate for taking action to improve nutrition. However, it is apparent that political leaders will not judge the effectiveness of these sectors based on their success in reducing the prevalence of undernutrition in the population. Other criteria than undernutrition are used to assess their effective-

ness, reducing the incentives for their prioritizing action to address undernutrition.

Although progress has been made in developing institutional mechanisms to coordinate the nutrition actions of government and NGOs in all of the countries except Ghana, there is far less evidence of any progress in ensuring that substantial, sustained allocations of state resources are made to assist the undernourished. Without the allocation of such resources, substantial reductions in the numbers of undernourished in each country are unlikely in the short to medium term, and the institutions that have been established to coordinate nutrition action using these resources are unlikely to be able to justify their continued existence.

In all four countries, there is a limited understanding among political leaders and policymakers of both the costs of aggregate undernutrition in the country for national development and of the determinants of nutritional status. Once the costs of undernutrition are perceived, an understanding of the determinants of improved nutrition is needed to guide action. This requirement is evident in the limited linking of any policy narratives on undernutrition to master development narratives in the country. Indeed, in several of the countries, the national nutrition policies that have been developed do not make a good case for why undernutrition should be seen as a development problem, in addition to being a human rights issue.

The argument made in this report is that food security is an element of nutrition security, as the determinants of improved nutrition go well beyond food. However, in all four countries, food security and nutrition security are not clearly distinguished, but are conflated to some degree. Consequently, even if the population is better fed because of the implementation of the various food and nutrition policies, the policies are not sufficiently clear on the multiple causes of undernutrition to ensure substantial improvements in nutritional status.

Similarly, virtually all interviewees recognized the importance of gender perspec-

Table 5.2 Characteristics of nutrition in policy processes across study countries

Issue	Ghana	Mozambique	Nigeria	Uganda
Key policymaking structures	General policymaking structures run from the Council of Ministers through the National Development Planning Commission and the Ministry of Finance and Economic Planning to the sectoral ministries. However, nutrition does not feature prominently at any level.	Ministry of Planning and Finance coordinates policymaking. Ministries are responsible for sectoral policies. There is cross-sectoral formulation of nutrition policy, although nutrition activities, narrowly defined, fall within the health sector. International agencies are important for policy implementation.	Centralized and personalized in the office of the president. There have been recent efforts to increase role of sectoral ministries in priority setting. Although NPC is potentially central to some policymaking processes, the NCFN is peripheral to these processes.	Centered on the office of the president, with sectoral ministries responsible for technical content. Policy coordination is done by the Ministry of Finance. Ambitious, if still weak, decentralization of government policymaking functions is taking place.
Key actors for nutrition policy	There is little action on setting priorities. Head of Nutrition Unit of Ghana Health Service is the most significant actor for policy implementation.	Development of food security and nutrition policy is due more to efforts of key actors in Ministries of Planning and Finance and Health than for structural reasons. Few nutrition advocates now remain in national policy processes.	No nutrition actors are participating in central policy processes. Members of NCFN and the allied Nutrition Partners group could be key advocates for nutrition policy in broader policy processes.	There have been some past policy champions for nutrition. Now key administrators within the PMA secretariat and members of the UFNC are key actors.
Key narratives on nutrition as a policy problem	Poverty reduction is a key development policy narrative. No narrative storylines effectively link improved nutrition to economic growth and poverty reduction. Nutrition is seen as a routine concern of the health sector; broader determinants of nutritional status are not apparent in policy on nutrition.	Nutrition policy is framed within a food security context, which provides insufficient guidance on the range of actions needed to reduce undernutrition.	Formal policy narratives are poorly developed, given the weakness of policy in government priority setting. Nutrition receives some priority in broad policy as an element of human rights. Policy on food and nutrition emphasizes the importance of good nutrition as a precondition for human development.	Nutrition largely absent in PEAP, the master development framework, or in the PMA. The Uganda Food and Nutrition Policy does not link undernutrition to government's broader development objectives. Decentralized policymaking on nutrition is hampered by limited understanding of the burden of undernutrition and the remedial actions needed.
Circumstances favorable for nutrition policy change	Nutrition priorities are treated within a bureaucratic framework. Regular reviews of the Ghana poverty reduction strategy, the master development framework, offer the possibility for policy change in nutrition.	Regular reviews of PARPA, the master development framework, offer the possibility for policy change in nutrition. Implementation of national food security and nutrition strategy is problematic for nutrition, which may force a reformulation of policy.	Change in country leadership tends to bring broad policy changes. However, in order for nutrition priorities to advance during regime change, strategic advocacy is required. International policy narratives may influence attention paid to undernutrition.	Regular reviews of PEAP are undertaken. International initiatives influence attention paid to undernutrition. Evolving political landscape may lead to an increased ability to raise the profile of undernutrition as a development problem.

Notes: NCFN is National Committee on Food and Nutrition; NPC is National Planning Commission; PEAP is Poverty Eradication Action Plan; PMA is Plan for the Modernisation of Agriculture; UFNC is Uganda Food and Nutrition Council.

tives in nutrition policy formulation and program design, attitudes that were considerably different from those predominant in the study countries. However, examples of the effective use of gender analysis in such efforts were rare.

A common pattern in all four countries is that coordination does not occur across sectors in developing programs to address undernutrition. The conceptual framework of the determinants of nutritional status in Figure 3.2 highlights the multisectoral nature of the underlying determinants of nutritional status. Among the rationales for establishing the various food and nutrition councils in Mozambique, Nigeria, and Uganda was to ensure effective coordination of efforts to reduce undernutrition. Although all these councils are too new to have established much of a record of accomplishment, the experience so far is not encouraging. Certainly in the case of Mozambique, the sectors involved seem to view coordination of activities to be a zero-sum gain in which any resources given up by one sector to support a broader, coordinated cross-sectoral effort are judged to be a net loss to that sector, and no advantages accrue to the sector through coordinated efforts with others.

Finally, the actors who are directly involved with nutrition advocacy and the coordination of nutrition activities present some common patterns across the countries, in terms of both who does and who does not participate. International partners, whether donors or NGOs, tend to be important partners in nutrition-focused activities and their coordination. This is especially the case in Mozambique, but can be seen in all of the countries. On the other hand, there is seemingly little engagement by national civil groups in nutrition advocacy. This failure likely reflects a combination of a lack of advocacy to engage existing civil groups on this issue and simply a lack of public awareness of the costs of undernutrition and how to address the problem. Finally, in the government sectors engaged in nutrition coordi-

nation activities, given the multisectoral nature of the determinants of nutritional status, there are commonly several missing participants—most notably the water, sanitation, and housing sectors, as well as community and local government organizations.

Differences

The countries differ in the prominence of formal policymaking to guide resource allocations by government. Nigeria stands in contrast to the other three countries. Differences in this regard are reflected in the transparency of the policymaking process, the predictability of government priorities over the longer term, and the degree to which technical policy research might be used to guide priority setting. These differences are important in considering how nutrition advocates might successfully engage in efforts to raise the profile of nutrition as a policy issue. Bureaucratic approaches along sectoral lines may prove effective in those countries with more structured policy processes. In countries with disorganized policy processes, a more personal approach using policy champions may be effective. However, in evaluating the degree to which the state meets the needs of the undernourished so far, it is unclear whether these differences in the quality of the policy processes in the four countries are significant.

The countries also differ in the level of expertise that they have in addressing problems of nutrition. Mozambique has very few professional nutritionists, while Nigeria has many hundreds. However, there is little evidence that the prospects for the undernourished in Nigeria are any better than in Mozambique. The manner in which available human capacity in nutrition is used is certainly as important as the presence of trained nutritionists.

Where policymaking is centralized, a few motivated nutritionists are adequate to provide policymakers with the necessary nutrition analyses and technical inputs to guide the formulation of policy and the allocation of resources across the sectors. However, where policymaking is decentralized and develops in a bottom-up manner, the constraints in human capacity in nutrition are much more salient. The study countries differ significantly in their commitments to fostering decentralized policymaking. Although none have in place strong local government systems, Uganda has made the most progress in this regard. There it is becoming clear that for local governments to take action to address the needs of the undernourished among their citizens, they must be provided with considerably more information on the costs of the problem at the community and subcounty level and what needs to be done to reduce it. For this effort, local governments will need more technical support from nutritionists.

Finally, although undernutrition has not been advanced effectively as a priority policy problem in any of the countries, Ghana is the one study country in which there is least evidence of action in this regard. However, Ghana has the lowest prevalence of child undernutrition across the four countries. Although the nutrition policy efforts in the other study countries are too recent to offer valid counterfactuals, Ghana's pattern of treating undernutrition as a routine primary health care problem could be considered an adequate approach to containing levels of undernutrition. However, the sharp increases in the prevalence of stunted children between 1988 and 2003 calls into question the business-as-usual approach to addressing undernutrition in Ghana. Maintaining the prevalence of stunted children at 20 percent or higher is indicative of success in addressing undernutrition.

The above summary ends the discussion of the findings from the institutional study in Ghana, Mozambique, Nigeria, and Uganda on what it is about national policymaking, nutrition, and nutrition in the context of policymaking that makes it difficult for undernutrition to be targeted as a national development priority. In the final chapter, I examine in a more prescriptive fashion how increases in the allocations of public resources to assist the undernourished in the four countries might be achieved.

CHAPTER 6

Prospects for Increasing Allocations of Public Resources to Improve Nutrition

All four study countries face continuing challenges in addressing undernutrition. None has succeeded in putting in place policy mechanisms to reduce sustainably the numbers of the undernourished in their populations. As can be seen in Figure 6.1, the prevalence of stunted and underweight children less than 3 years of age has not been reduced substantially in any of the four countries over the past 15 to 20 years, although a recent decline in the level of stunting in Uganda is encouraging. Given that between one-quarter and one-third of all children in these countries are stunted in their physical growth and cognitive development, the human costs of undernutrition in these countries are immense. Certainly, the governments of the study countries are not effectively addressing the human right to adequate nutrition for these children. Of equal significance, the development objectives of economic growth and poverty reduction that these countries share are hampered by the compromised economic potential of so many members of their populations from birth caused by their own and their mothers' undernutrition.

Nor is it clear that any of these governments are now making substantial efforts to reduce undernutrition. The problem receives little, if any, attention as a key constraint to human and economic development. Consequently, allocations of government resources to address undernutrition are limited. On most criteria for addressing undernutrition as a public policy problem, none of the four study countries can be judged as successful, given the size of the problem they are facing. Although small positive steps can be identified in all, much more effort is needed.

In this chapter, I use the findings from the four study countries presented in the previous chapter to suggest how action might be taken so that substantially reducing levels of undernutrition in the population is treated by government as a primary objective.

Summary of Study Findings

The research on nutrition in the policy process of the four countries shows a consistent pattern of the national governments paying some attention to the problem of undernutrition, but not enough to substantially reduce the levels of undernutrition seen in their populations. In all of the study countries, regardless of the degree to which formal policy statements guide government decisionmaking, the commitment to broad human development, or the levels of undernutrition observed, undernutrition tends to be treated as a business-as-usual issue. There is no drama associated with it; no concern that the issue is critical to the future of the country and the well-being of its citizens. There is relatively poor linking of the problem of undernutrition to the achievement of the master development objectives of the government. In only one or

Figure 6.1   Trends in the prevalence of stunted and underweight children less than 3 years of age in the study countries

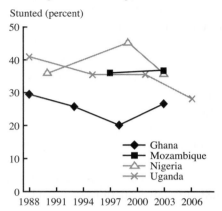

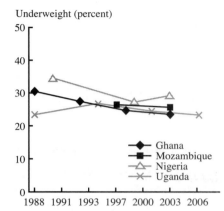

Source: Data from ORC/Macro (2007).

two of the nutrition policies is improved nutrition noted as being both an important output of development efforts and a critical input to achieve the broad development goals of economic growth and poverty reduction. National and sectoral policy statements are silent, offering no perspectives on the importance of nutrition in attaining their objectives. Formal policy statements do not feature prominently in setting the scope and scale of government action or in allocating public resources to address undernutrition.

Rather, existing sectoral mandates tend to be used to determine what public actions are needed and assign responsibility for carrying them out. There is no coordination of these efforts to ensure that actions are properly sequenced or that all elements needed to improve the nutritional status of the population are in place. As shown by the unproductive discussions in Uganda over several decades on where in government nutrition should officially be located, when any debates on nutrition-related issues in the public sector occur, they primarily seem to be over the allocation of potentially new public resources provided for such efforts. Yet for all the sectors concerned, whether health, education, agriculture, water and sanitation, or any others, nutrition activities are viewed as secondary priorities and im-

proved nutrition outcomes as secondary sectoral objectives.

It is unlikely that a change in the priority accorded nutrition issues in these countries will occur without efforts to raise the profile of undernutrition as a significant problem that the government must address. However, nutrition advocacy organizations in these countries are absent in most cases or embryonic, at best. Although nutrition coordination councils have been established in three of the four countries, in none is it yet clear how they are to engage in the relevant policy and resource allocation processes to ensure that government as a whole and the individual sectors act to combat undernutrition successfully. The absence of effective nutrition advocacy coalitions in the four study countries appears to be a key constraint on building the commitment of government to assist the undernourished attain nutrition security by providing them with nutrition-related goods and services. There is little demand on governments to account for continuing high levels of undernutrition in their populations.

In the remainder of this chapter, I examine the issue of advocacy for increased attention by the state to the problem of undernutrition. The discussion is structured as in other chapters by considering, first, who should be the target of advocacy efforts—that is, what policymaking structures or policymakers are of most relevance. Second, I consider who might undertake these advocacy efforts. Who are the key actors that can be expected to engage policymakers effectively? Finally, I consider the advocacy message or narrative that they might employ.

Who Should Be the Focus of Efforts to Change Policy on Nutrition?

In terms of the advocacy that might be undertaken to foster policy change and the target of the advocacy efforts, the perspective one adopts in seeking to understand the policy processes in these countries matters. This report has shown that a state-centered approach to understanding policymaking and policy change, focusing on policy elites primarily in government, has proven more insightful in explaining the level of attention given to undernutrition as a policy problem in these countries than does a society-centered approach. The impact of this perspective on advocacy is that, as Grindle and Thomas note (1989, 244, footnote 5):

> Promoters of reform who adopt a society-centered explanation of policy, for example, would be well advised to concentrate efforts on mobilizing interest group activities or attempting to create coalitions and alliances of classes and interests to influence authoritative decision making by government. If, on the other hand, a state-centered explanation of policy is adopted, reformers might better concentrate effort on directly influencing the perceptions of decision makers about the goals and content of policy.

Consequently, in the study countries and similar developing nations, nutrition advocates are likely to achieve the greatest payoff in terms of policy change for a given effort if they target senior political and bureaucratic decisionmakers. These policy elites determine what issues are included in the policymaking agenda at any point in time, manage the formulation of policy, and oversee the implementation of those policies. Engaging with these individuals to change their understanding of the significance of undernutrition as a problem demanding public action has strategic potential for altering the level of engagement of government.

In all four countries at present, it is primarily mid-level administrators and technicians in the state who are managing policy debates on nutrition issues. This situation reflects, as noted earlier, the manner in which undernutrition is perceived as a policy issue. Because high levels of undernutrition are seen to be an undesirable but longstanding characteristic of each of these countries, it is judged a sufficient response that bureaucratic processes already in place be adapted to undertake action to address or, at least, contain the problem of undernutrition. The managers of these nutrition-oriented activities in government likely are well aware of the impact of undernutrition on the well-being of individuals and their households and, in aggregate, on the prospects for substantial human and economic development for the country in the medium term. Moreover, they probably have quite a good idea of what needs to be done to reduce significantly levels of undernutrition in the population. However, they do not have sufficient power to determine the priorities of government on how its resources are allocated. The policy elites with this power are situated above them in the hierarchies of government. As such, these managers and technocrats are better seen as allies in advocacy efforts than as important targets for those efforts and should be explicitly included in the formation of any advocacy coalitions formed to promote action to reduce levels of undernutrition.

An important contextual element in determining who among the policy elite should be targeted by advocates is the importance of explicit policy statements to guide resource allocations by a government. Where such statements are important, technical arguments and an understanding of the institutional mechanisms for engaging in policy processes are likely useful for conducting effective advocacy. However, where priorities are established in a less transparent fashion, personalized policymaking is the norm. In such governments, political considerations tend to trump arguments on technical efficiency and the cultivation of key political leaders as policy champions is a necessary component of an advocacy effort. The weight accorded the opinions of sectoral managers and senior technicians in policy debates in such politically charged policymaking is likely to be less than where there is a strong technocratic element in the process. It is advantageous to cultivate policy champions for combating undernutrition in all policymaking contexts, but it is more of a necessity where the policymaking mechanisms are less clearly defined.

Finally, in considering the focus of efforts to bring about policy change in nutrition, there is merit in raising the awareness of the general public of the burdens of undernutrition and what can be done to reduce this burden. This effort can be done in formal ways, such as teaching public health and nutrition topics in primary and secondary schools or discussing behavior changes at health clinics or in community groups, or in informal ways using mass media. Doing so is useful in its own right to increase understanding of the importance of good nutrition and what constitutes good nutritional care. More importantly, raising awareness also develops a foundation for political dialogue about undernutrition at local levels. Particularly where, as in Uganda, there are mechanisms for bottom-up policymaking, increased public understanding of the causes of undernutrition is necessary for building pressure on local political leaders to support government efforts to reduce levels of undernutrition. Although broad awareness-raising efforts will not alter government policy in the short term, over time such efforts will increase expectations that government has a responsibility for ensuring that all citizens are properly nourished.

Who Should Act?

Who should advocate for increased attention to the problem of undernutrition, engage in policy processes, and hold leaders and policymakers accountable? Given the poor fit of nutrition across the sectors of government and the consequent problems for establishing leadership on the issue, a national advocacy coalition should be formed around the issue of undernutrition. Such coalitions will be made up of individuals from government, civil society, international agencies, and private institutions in the nation who share a set of basic beliefs on undernutrition both as an issue of human rights and as a concern for human and economic development. The members of the advocacy coalition should work in as coordinated a fashion as possible to focus attention on the problem of undernutrition by government and increase the level of resources it allocates to address the problem. In the four study countries, the example of the Nutrition Partners group in Nigeria is the closest to what is envisioned here.

The advocacy coalition proposed draws upon those described by Jenkins-Smith and Sabatier (1993, 5) in their Advocacy Coalition Framework (ACF) model of policy change, except that the policy subsystem of interest here, that of undernutrition, more than likely will only have the single advocacy coalition operating within it—what the authors elsewhere call a "nascent" policy subsystem (Sabatier and Jenkins-Smith 1999, 135ff.). The ACF model is a society-centered explanation of policymaking that posits opposing advocacy coalitions at the center of any action in a policy subsystem. Given how the policy process operates in the study countries and the limited attention that undernutrition has received in them to date, it is unlikely that separate advocacy coalitions will emerge with sufficiently distinct viewpoints on undernutrition to lead to the formation of opposing political groups.

Given the problem of establishing policy leadership on the issue of undernutrition, the creation of such coalitions is problematic. No clear guidance can be provided here. To some degree, leadership for and participation in such advocacy efforts will depend on chance and the personal qualities of the participants—their training, experience, personal values, and vision—that would lead them to involvement in such advocacy efforts. However, such processes can be seeded. A typical pattern seems to be that topical nutrition concerns—such as international pressure to formulate national food and nutrition strategies—provide a kernel of a group of nutrition advocates whose membership and functions can then be expanded. The multisectoral nutrition coordination bodies that have been established in several of the study countries provide the basis for the creation of parallel and more broadly based advocacy coalitions. In Nigeria, the Nutrition Partners group emerged principally from broader consultations and interest in the National Policy on Food and Nutrition and its action plan that went beyond the relatively narrow and government-centered committee established by the policy. Additionally, international development partners backed the creation of such a body to facilitate their own support of nutrition activities in Nigeria, providing incentives for the continued interaction of the group members. There is a need for regular interaction if the coalition is to cohere and develop a common advocacy message.

Mainstreaming of attention to nutrition in policy processes and sectoral action should be a key aim of the advocacy coalition. This effort can range from simple information sharing and raising public awareness about undernutrition as a policy problem to actual engagement in political debates to establish priorities for government action on nutrition. As de Haan (2002,

33) notes, "the main challenge for this may well not be in the theoretical arguments, but in the day-to-day processes of policy making, inclusiveness of debates, and capacities to engage across the boundaries of sectors, departments, or communities." To attain its objectives, a nutrition advocacy coalition will need to undertake a detailed assessment of the political landscape and the circumstances and policymakers that present useful opportunities for engaging in the policy process. Using this information to develop a realistic advocacy strategy, coalition members can then be given appropriate responsibilities to see that the strategy is implemented.

The previous section emphasized that mid-level administrators and technicians in government who are responsible for nutrition-oriented activities are better viewed as fellow advocates in efforts to raise the profile of nutrition in national policy processes than as targets of advocacy. They should be brought into any advocacy coalition, given the centrality of their agencies to any government action to address undernutrition. However, there will be limits on their participation in and leadership of the advocacy activities of the coalition because of their functional dependency on the bureaucrats and political leaders who will be among the principal advocacy targets for the coalition (Sabatier and Jenkins-Smith 1999, 141).

Although the multisectoral nutrition coordination bodies that have been set up by government might provide an initial focal point for the creation of such advocacy coalitions, it is less clear what the role of such councils should be for advocacy. In many cases, they will not be able to exercise any advocacy functions. In other cases, they may be given some formal oversight on how the sectors involved in addressing undernutrition perform. In such cases, it is also more likely that they will be included in policy discussions related to undernutrition. Overall, the study of the three countries with such councils shows that there is no specific recipe for how they can be made to function effectively. Their ability to raise the profile of undernutrition as a policy problem and increase funding for it depends on their institutional profile in the sectors concerned and with policymakers, the personal characteristics of their leadership, and the support they receive from political leaders. From an advocacy standpoint, their position will vary from country to country—in some being useful partners in advocacy, in others possibly being targets of advocacy efforts.

What Is the Message?

The nature and causes of undernutrition and the magnitude of its costs to society are not adequately recognized by most policymakers. This ignorance poses a major obstacle to building demand for action against it and must be directly addressed through advocacy efforts. Undernutrition is often hidden. It requires knowledge to identify the threat and to advocate appropriate action against it. Much of the preparatory work of an advocacy coalition that seeks to engage strategically with the policy elite on nutrition consists of developing a convincing and tractable definition of the problem of undernutrition (Hajer 1995, 15).

A clear presentation on the costs of undernutrition to the country is necessary to goad policymakers into action. Providing an instrumental understanding of the severity of the problem is likely be the most effective approach. That is, the problem should be couched in a framework that incorporates the master development objectives of the country, whether economic growth, poverty reduction, or other objectives, and demonstrate to political leaders how those objectives are not likely to be attained if the constraints on development efforts imposed by undernutrition are not removed.

The importance of gendered perspectives in the design and implementation of nutrition policy should also be a subtheme of such advocacy messages. Gender analysis as a tool in all policy processes, whether focused on nutrition or otherwise, is still an abstract concept in most people's minds. Because the adverse effects of gender inequities on the quality of nutritional care and, thus, on nutritional status, are quite clear, incorporating gender analyses into nutrition policy processes will enhance the quality of the resultant nutrition policy and the efficiency with which it is implemented. Incorporation will also demonstrate the usefulness of gender analysis in policy processes. More importantly, the development and implementation of gender-sensitive nutrition policies will contribute in a small but tangible manner to broader aims of reducing inequalities between men and women in society.

Advocates should not ignore broad normative imperatives centered on human rights to ensure that all individuals are properly nourished. If it is the right thing to do and it can be done, then most policy elites and their constituents would agree that it should be done. At the core of the problem of undernutrition is a human dimension, and the advocacy message should transparently demonstrate how public action will result in improved nutritional status and a better life for the individual child or woman, in particular.

Having understood the message that undernutrition is a substantial problem for human welfare and development, policymakers will require guidance on action. Advocates should ensure that policymakers have a set of tools to employ once they agree that government must prioritize action to address undernutrition. The provision of a relatively simple conceptual framework of the determinants of nutritional status, such as that presented in Figure 3.2, is a useful device to enable policymakers to identify who needs to act and the priorities of their actions. Moreover, such a framework can be used to clarify misconceptions on the nature of the problem, such as the commonly seen conflation of food security with nutrition security. Although more detailed analysis is needed of particular problems to design programs tailored to a specific country, the conceptual framework provides the decisionmakers with a useful guide for addressing the problem in general.

To formulate or revise existing sectoral policies for master development, advocates for nutrition should present clear and consistent messages of the roles that the government and each sector should play in reducing undernutrition in a concerted and harmonized manner. The objective is to make government and its various sectoral agencies recognize the importance of their efforts to assist the undernourished and to build a sense of responsibility in government for making these efforts.

Finally, advocates should make a strong case for why government needs to involve itself in actions to reduce the level of undernutrition in the population. Advocates should recognize that the nutritional status of a young child is the immediate outcome of principally household-level processes and conditions. However, there is much that the government must do to enable households to provide for their own nutritional needs. The responsibility for the provision of many of the key goods and services that enable household members to provide proper nutritional care for themselves— appropriate education on nutritional care, health services, safe water, improving the stability of household access to food, and so on—principally lies with government.

To conclude, in discussing the persistence of hunger in the world, Sen (1999, 204) also provides a critique, by extension, of persisting high levels of undernutrition:

> The contemporary age is not short
> of terrible and nasty happenings,
> but the persistence of extensive
> hunger in a world of unprecedented
> prosperity is surely one of the
> worst. . . . What makes this wide-

spread hunger even more of a tragedy is the way we have come to accept and tolerate it as an integral part of the modern world, as if it is a tragedy that is essentially unpreventable.

The principal challenge in addressing undernutrition as a policy problem is that in most developing nations, a high prevalence of undernutrition in the population is not seen as anomalous and indicative of the inability of the government to fulfill its duties to its citizens. Undernutrition is not identified as being among those priority problems that the state must address with urgency if it is to safeguard its legitimacy.

Nutrition advocates must seek to alter this perception of undernutrition as being a characteristic of the normal order of things. In carrying out their advocacy, they should generate a perception of crisis related to undernutrition to foster significant, urgent, high-profile action by government. However, typically the qualitative change in the perception of nutritional conditions in a country to one of crisis cannot be sustained in the long term. As priorities of government change and new crises arise, undernutrition as a policy problem reverts to being perceived as an element of politics-as-usual (Grindle and Thomas 1991, 190). Nevertheless, at least incremental changes in the profile of the policy problem of undernutrition can be sustained and exploited, so that more effective actions are taken to assist the undernourished. Because undernutrition is a solvable problem that, in part, requires public action to address sustainably, governments should and can be held accountable for the persistent presence of undernourished women and children in the population, the unnecessary suffering they experience, and the limited potential that they have to live long, healthy, productive, and creative lives.

APPENDIX A

Interviewees

Ghana

Head
Nutrition Unit
Ghana Health Service
Accra

Pro-vice-chancellor
University for Development Studies
Tamale

Manager for farmer-based organizations
Women in Agricultural Development
    Department (WIAD)
Ministry of Food and Agriculture
Accra

Nutrition advisor
Basic Support for Institutionalizing Child
    Survival (BASICS II) project
Accra

Assistant director
Policy, Planning, Monitoring, and
    Evaluation Division (PPMED)
Ministry of Food and Agriculture
Accra

National child health coordinator
Reproductive and Child Health Unit
Ministry of Health
Accra

Director
Policy, Planning, Monitoring, and
    Evaluation Division (PPMED)
Ministry of Health
Accra

Health desk officer
Ministry of Finance and Economic
    Planning
Accra

Coordinator
Community-Based Poverty Reduction
    Project (CPRP)
National Development Planning
    Commission
Accra

Acting director
Policy, Planning, Monitoring and
    Evaluation
Ministry for Women and Children's Affairs
Accra

Program manager, health
Catholic Relief Services—Ghana
Accra

Technical coordinator—health
Adventist Development and Relief Agency
Accra

Nutrition development and gender officer
Adventist Development and Relief Agency
Accra

Program coordinator
National Capacity Building Programme for
    Wealth Creation and Social
    Development
National Development Planning
    Commission
Accra

Program officer, nutrition
UNICEF
Accra

Monitoring and evaluation officer
Linkages Project—Ghana
Accra

Acting director and technical advisor and
    training officer
Linkages Project—Ghana
Accra

Deputy director
Noguchi Memorial Institute for Medical
    Research
University of Ghana
Accra

Head
Department of Nutrition and Food Science
University of Ghana—Legon
Accra

Senior lecturer
Department of Nutrition and Food Science
University of Ghana—Legon
Accra

Regional human resource development
    officer
Ministry of Food and Agriculture—
    Central Region
Cape Coast

Regional nutrition officer
Ghana Health Service—Central Region
Cape Coast

District development officer for
    agriculture, responsible for WIAD
Komenda, Edina, Eguafo, Abrem District

Deputy district coordinating director
Komenda, Edina, Eguafo, Abrem District
    Assembly
Elmina

District nutrition officer
Ghana Health Service
Komenda, Edina, Eguafo, Abrem District

Regional director of food and agriculture
Central Region
Cape Coast

District director of health services
Komenda, Edina, Eguafo, Abrem District,
    Central Region
Elmina

National program officer
Integrated Management of Childhood
    Illness
World Health Organization—Ghana
Accra

Micronutrients and Health (MICAH)
    project manager
World Vision—Ghana
Mpraeso, Eastern Region

Nutrition and food security desk officer
Women in Agricultural Development
    (WIAD) Directorate
Ministry of Food and Agriculture
Accra

Head
Gender and Inequality Section
Policy Unit
Policy, Planning, Monitoring and
    Evaluation Directorate
Ghana Health Service
Accra

Director/representative
World Food Programme
Accra

Director
Directorate of Agricultural Extension
    Services
Ministry of Food and Agriculture
Accra

Senior lecturer–nutritionist/home
    economist
Home Science Department
University of Ghana—Legon
Accra

Senior regional food and nutrition officer
Head of Economic and Social Department
    Group
Regional Office for Africa
Food and Agriculture Organization of the
    United Nations
Accra

Director
Technology Consultancy Centre
Kwame Nkrumah University of Science
    and Technology
Kumasi

Director
Policy, Planning, Monitoring and
    Evaluation Directorate (PPMED)
Ghana Health Service
Accra

Mozambique

Country representative
Helen Keller International
Maputo

Agricultural economist
National Directorate of Livestock
Ministry of Agriculture and Rural
    Development (MADER)
Maputo

Country project director
Southern Africa Root Crops Research
    Network (SAARNET)
Maputo

Agro-business consultant
TechnoServe Mozambique
Maputo

Forestry specialist
TechnoServe Mozambique
Maputo

Agricultural services specialist
Mozambique Resident Mission
World Bank
Maputo

Nutritionist
Nutrition Section
Ministry of Health
Maputo

Agriculture and Food for Peace staff (five
    individuals)
United States Agency for International
    Development (USAID)
Maputo

Coordenador do Secretariado Técnico de
    Segurança Alimentar e Nutrição
    (SETSAN) Central
Direcção Nacional de Agricultura
Ministry of Agriculture and Rural
    Development (MADER)
Maputo

Coordenador do Sistema Nacional de
    Coordenação de Aviso Prévio
    (SENCAP)/Secretariado Técnico de
    Segurança Alimentar e Nutrição
    (SETSAN)
Direcção Nacional de Agricultura
Ministry of Agriculture and Rural
    Development (MADER)
Maputo

Economist
Direcção Nacional do Plano e Orcamento
Ministerio do Plano e Financas
Maputo

Nutritionist
Associação Nutrição e Segurança
    Alimentar (ANSA)
Maputo

Director nacional
Direcçào Nactional do Comércio
Ministério da Indústria e Comércio
    (MIC)
Maputo

Chefe do departamento
Departamento de Produçào Agrícola
Direcçào Nacional de Agricultura
Ministry of Agriculture and Rural
    Development (MADER)
Maputo

Scientist in biology
Instituto Nacional de Investigaçào
    Agronómica (National Institute of
    Agronomic Research)
Maputo

Gender focal point
Instituto Nacional de Investigaçào
    Agronómica (National Institute of
    Agronomic Research)
Maputo

Soil fertility agronomist
Land and Water Department
Instituto Nacional de Investigaçào
    Agronómica (National Institute of
    Agronomic Research)
Maputo

Program officer
Danish International Development
    Assistance (Danida)—Apoio ao
    programa do sector agrário
Agricultural Sector Public Expenditure
    Program (PROAGRI)/Direcçào
    Nacional de Economia
Ministry of Agriculture and Rural
    Development (MADER)
Maputo

Chief technical advisor
Projecto de Assistência à Gestão do
    Mercado
Direcçào Nactional do Comércio
Ministério da Indústria e Comércio
Maputo

Health and nutrition director
World Vision
Maputo

Deputy director of agriculture
World Vision
Maputo

National director of agriculture
Direcçào Nacional de Agricultura
Ministry of Agriculture and Rural
    Development (MADER)
Maputo

Vice-Ministro
Ministry of Agriculture and Rural
    Development (MADER)
Maputo

Agricultural economist/statistician
Faculty of Agronomy and Forest
    Engineering
University Eduardo Mondlane
Maputo

Coordinator
Mozambique Integrated Information
    Network for Decision-Making
    (MIND)
Maputo

Vulnerability specialist
Famine Early Warning System (FEWS)
Maputo

Designated country representative
Famine Early Warning System (FEWS)
Maputo

Head
Departamento de Apoio Técnico
Direcçào Nacional de Extensão Rural
Ministry of Agriculture and Rural
    Development (MADER)
Maputo

Sociologist
Centre of African Studies
University Eduardo Mondlane
Maputo

Representative in Mozambique and
    Swaziland
Food and Agriculture Organization of the
    United Nations
Maputo

Natural resources and gender specialist
Food and Agriculture Organization of the
    United Nations
Maputo

Head
Departamento de Aviso Prévio
Direcçao Nacional de Agricultura
Ministry of Agriculture and Rural
    Development (MADER)
Maputo

Acting country director
Africare
Maputo

Epidemiologist
Ministry of Health
Chókwè

Coordinator
Integrated Rural Development Project
    Chókwè—Gaza Province
Lutheran World Federation—Mozambique
    Programme
Chókwè

Director of Chókwè District
Ministry of Agriculture and Rural
    Development (MADER)
Chókwè

Scientist
Mozambique Food Security Project
Michigan State University
Quelimane

Nigeria

Head
Nutrition Unit
Public Health Division
Lagos State Ministry of Health
Ikeja, Lagos

Principal nutritionist
Nutrition Division
Federal Ministry of Health
Lagos

Higher nutrition officer
Nutrition Division
Federal Ministry of Health
Lagos

Principal nutrition officer
Nutrition Division
Federal Ministry of Health
Lagos

Integrated management of childhood
    illnesses program officer
World Health Organization, Nigeria
Yaba, Lagos

Nutrition programme officer
World Health Organization, Nigeria
Yaba, Lagos

Head
Department of Nutrition and Dietetics
University of Nigeria Teaching Hospital—
    Enugu
Enugu

Head
Department of Agriculture
Oshimili North Local Government Council
Local Government Secretariat
Akwukwu-Igbo, Delta State

Professor
Department of Human Nutrition
University of Agriculture—Abeokuta
Abeokuta, Ogun State

Professor
Department of Human Nutrition
University of Ibadan
Ibadan, Oyo State

Professor
Department of Home Science and
    Nutrition
University of Nigeria—Nsukka
Nsukka, Enugu State

Lecturer
Department of Home Science and
    Nutrition
University of Nigeria—Nsukka
Nsukka, Enugu State

Basic Support for Institutionalizing Child
    Survival (BASICS) project consultant
Badagry Local Government Authority
    (LGA) Headquarters Health Center
Badagry LGA
Lagos State

Family health services officer
Badagry Local Government Authority
    (LGA) Headquarters Health Center
Badagry LGA
Lagos State

Nutrition officer
Badagry Local Government Authority
    (LGA)
Lagos State

Head
Department of Agriculture, Rural, and
    Social Development
Badagry Local Government Authority
    (LGA)
Lagos State

Chair, National Committee on Food and
  Nutrition and Head, Agriculture and
  Industry Department
National Planning Commission
Abuja

Principal nutrition officer
National Primary Health Care
  Development Agency
Abuja

Economist
Poverty Alleviation Department
National Planning Commission
Abuja

Head
Nutrition Unit
UNICEF
Abuja

Nutrition officer
United States Agency for International
  Development (USAID)
Abuja

Agriculture development officer
United States Agency for International
  Development (USAID)
Abuja

Special assistant to the director general
International Institute of Tropical
  Agriculture
Ibadan

Principal administrative officer
Department of Planning, Research and
  Statistics
Federal Ministry of Women's Affairs and
  Youth Development
Abuja

Home economist
Technology and Science Education
  Department
Federal Ministry of Education
Abuja

Assistant director
External Relations and Special Projects
Department of Agriculture

Federal Ministry of Agriculture and Rural
  Development
Abuja

Chief nutritionist and desk officer for
  gender and women's health
Division of Reproductive Health
Department of Community Development
  and Population Activities
Federal Ministry of Health
Abuja

Assistant chief nutrition officer
Borno State Ministry of Health
Maiduguri, Borno State

Head
Skills Development, Training, and
  Nutrition Division
Federal Department of Rural Development
Federal Ministry of Agriculture and Rural
  Development
Abuja

Rural livelihoods adviser
Department for International Development
British High Commission
Abuja

Director
Federal Department of Rural Development
Federal Ministry of Agriculture and Rural
  Development
Abuja

Uganda
Principal research officer
Kawanda Agricultural Research Institute
National Agricultural Research
  Organization
Kampala

Planning, monitoring and evaluation
  manager
National Agricultural Advisory Services
  Secretariat
Kampala

Lecturer
Women and Gender Studies Department
Makerere University
Kampala

Acting principal gender officer
Ministry of Gender, Labour, and Social
   Development
Kampala

Health specialist
World Bank
Kampala

Senior administrative officer
Ministry of Local Government
Kampala

Senior veterinary officer
Animal production and marketing
Ministry of Agriculture, Animal Industry,
   and Fisheries
Entebbe

Head
Home Economics and Nutrition
   Department
Ministry of Agriculture, Animal Industry,
   and Fisheries
Entebbe

Rural development specialist
World Bank
Kampala

Advisor
Plan for Modernisation of Agriculture
Ministry of Finance, Planning and
   Economic Development
Kampala

Head
Department of Food Science and
   Technology
Makerere University
Kampala

Programme officer—health and nutrition
United States Agency for International
   Development (USAID)
Kampala

Professor
Child Health and Development Center
Makerere University
Kampala

Desk officer
Ministry of Agriculture, Animal Industry,
   and Fisheries
Ministry of Finance, Planning and
   Economic Development
Kampala

Principal agricultural officer
Farm Development Department
Crop Directorate
Ministry of Agriculture, Animal Industry,
   and Fisheries
Entebbe

Executive director
National Agricultural Advisory Services
   Secretariat
Kampala

Coordinator for HIV/AIDS and agriculture
National Agricultural Advisory Services
   Secretariat
Kampala

President
Uganda National Farmers Federation
Kampala

Director of planning and technical services
Uganda National Farmers Federation
Kampala

Principal nutritionist
Nutrition Section
Child Health Division
Department of Community Health
Ministry of Health
Kampala

Director of health services
Luwero District
Luwero

Director of research
Namulonge Agricultural and Animal
   Production Research Institute
National Agricultural Research
   Organization
Kampala

Deputy director-general
National Agricultural Research Organization
Entebbe

Communication specialist
Nutrition and Early Childhood
    Development Project
Kampala

State minister (Entandikwa)
Ministry of Gender, Labour, and Social
    Development
Kampala

Programme officer—technical services
Plan for the Modernisation of Agriculture
    (PMA) Secretariat
Kampala

Coordinator
Food Security Program (Northern Uganda)
World Vision
Kampala

Counselor/development
Danish International Development
    Assistance (Danida)
Kampala

Program officer
Danish International Development
    Assistance (Danida)
Kampala

Head
Monitoring and Evaluation
The AIDS Support Organization (TASO)
Kampala

Director
Uganda National Health Research
    Organization
Entebbe

Deputy chief administrative officer
Luwero District
Luwero

Agriculture production officer
Luwero District
Luwero

Assistant community development officer
Luwero District
Luwero

Program officers (two individuals)
World Food Programme
Kampala

APPENDIX B

Sample Interview Guide for Institutional Study in Mozambique, Nigeria, and Uganda

This guide was used during the interviews conducted for the institutional study of agriculture and nutrition for the TANA project during fieldwork in Mozambique, Nigeria, and Uganda between September and November 2002. Separate guides were prepared for each country, with the only difference being that some of the questions were altered to better reflect the policy context and institutional organization of the public sector in the country. The interview guide used later in Ghana was modified substantially from this guide and is presented separately.

The documents were used as guides rather than as questionnaires. Consequently, the interviews were relatively unstructured in their flow, typically taking between 45 minutes and an hour to complete. The interview guides were used to ensure that all points that were considered relevant to the institutional study were covered in each interview, time allowing.

Introductory statement made to interviewee

The problem statement underlying the study is as follows:

The agriculture and nutrition communities are missing opportunities to more effectively reduce poverty, hunger, and malnutrition by failing to combine scarce resources, act together and, in part, to adequately incorporate gender analysis throughout their work.

This study is to examine how the agriculture and nutrition communities interact in [Mozambique/Nigeria/Uganda] and the policy processes fostering or constraining their interaction. The study will examine

- where agriculture and nutrition are located within the institutional arrangement of government,
- the professional formation and working conditions of agriculturalists and nutritionists and how these factors are reflected in their level of collaboration,
- how policies are made in [Mozambique/Nigeria/Uganda] and the priority accorded to agriculture and nutrition,
- the importance of nutrition in the formulation and implementation of the
  - [national plan for poverty reduction (PARPA), the sectoral public expenditure plan for agriculture (PROAGRI), and the National Food and Nutrition Security strategy (SETSAN) *(Moz.)*/
  - national development plans, sectoral public expenditure plans for agriculture, and national food and nutrition strategies *(Nig.)*/

- Poverty Eradication Action Plan (PEAP) and the Plan for Modernisation of Agriculture (PMA) *(Ug.)*], and
- the role which decentralization might play in improving nutrition *(Ug. only)*.

Underlying this study is the assertion that the social process through which agriculture and nutrition are linked—how food gets on the table and eaten—has an inherent gender element. Consequently, the study will explicitly examine the use made of gender analyses both in designing policies and in formulating activities that aim to improve the nutrition of [Mozambicans/Nigerians/Ugandans].

Two principal methods will be used—a close review of the literature on [Mozambican/Nigerian/Ugandan] government policy, agriculture, and nutrition, and interviews with key informants in [Mozambique/Nigeria/Uganda]. This questionnaire is to serve the latter method.

The key informants will be government policymakers, particularly those linked to the [PARPA and SETSAN/National Committee on Food and Nutrition/PEAP and PMA], as well as agriculturalists and nutritionists in government; academics in the fields of nutrition and agricultural research; the staff of nongovernmental organizations working in the area of food security, nutrition, and agriculture; and donors supporting such efforts in [Mozambique/Nigeria/Uganda]. The vast majority of the interviews will be carried out in [Maputo/Lagos and Abuja/Kampala and Entebbe].

Information on the respondent

- Position; Age; Sex; Training; Career path to this point; Likely future career path.
- Does position involve agriculture, nutrition, and the linkages between them in any way? If so, how?
  - Place of individual within an organogram of agriculture and nutrition institutions (formal and infor-

mal). *Ideally, ask the respondent to sketch out such an organogram.*

Nutritional status of [Mozambique's/Nigeria's/Uganda's] population

- Is malnutrition—whether hunger, insufficient calories or protein, or micronutrient deficiencies—perceived to be a problem in [Mozambique/Nigeria/Uganda] in general? If yes, describe the problem. What about if you look at the [province or district/state or Local Government Authority/district] level? What about within the population?
  - If no, would you give an assessment of how much this is due to conscious government policy and how much to [Mozambique/Nigeria/Uganda] being well endowed for productive agriculture?
- What institution(s) in government do you believe is/are responsible for the nutritional well-being of the population? Why? Why not agriculture, health, local government [delete as needed]?
- How do you find out about the nutritional status of [Mozambicans/Nigerians/Ugandans]? How available is this information?

Relationship between agriculture and nutrition in [Mozambique/Nigeria/Uganda]

- How would you characterize the professional relationship between nutritionists and agriculturalists in [Mozambique/Nigeria/Uganda]? What about that between health professionals and nutritionists?
  - *[If agriculturalist or nutritionist],* how much interaction do you have with specialists in the other field? Did you take courses or receive training with them? Do you attend workshops together?

- What are the central objectives of agriculturalist in their professional activities?
- How about for nutritionists?
- If you look at the interactions between agriculturalists and nutritionists at national, district, and community levels, is the quality of the interactions of the two groups similar regardless of the level at which they work?
  - Why is this the case? Are there any incentives (disincentives) in place at certain levels to encourage (impede) collaboration?
- In the formulation of government budgets, whether at national or district level, do nutritionists and agriculturalists tend to compete for the same funds or do they work in concert to get a larger slice of the budget for agriculture, food, and nutrition activities? Explain why this is so.
- What advantages or disadvantages might there be to greater cooperation between agriculturalists and nutritionists? Should they work together more closely? Benefits/costs of doing so?

Gender policy, agriculture, and nutrition in [Mozambique/Nigeria/Uganda]

- What are the gender issues that you face in your work?
  - Have you made use of gender analyses in planning your activities? If so, in what ways?
- In your view, how central are considerations of gender to how [Mozambican/Nigerian/Ugandan] agriculturalists carry out their activities? Why?
  - Are there any policy documents expecting that they use gender analysis in their work? *(Moz. & Nig.)*
  - The PMA requires that gender analysis and gender sensitive planning are made explicit components

of decision making to establish agricultural research and extension priorities. Does this work well in practice? Why? *(Ug.)*
- How central are gender considerations to how [Mozambican/Nigerian/Ugandan] nutritionists carry out their activities? Why?
- Do any examples of successful nutrition programs that linked agriculturalists with nutritionists come to mind? Briefly describe them.
  - Was gender analysis used in any way in the design or implementation of these programs?
- This study assumes that gender is a critical aspect of the process by which improved food production leads to better nutrition. Consequently, we promote the idea that gender should be a central component in the design and implementation of nutrition policies and programmes. What is your assessment of this perspective?
  - *If need to probe: Does this perspective state the obvious and so is meaningless? Or is it an uncommon, but important perspective? Or is it only one of several important aspects?*

Policy making in [Mozambique/Nigeria/Uganda]

- Could you describe how policy decisions are made in government?
  - Is this pattern seen at both national and district levels? If not, what differences?
- What are the basic motivations for most politicians taking action on policy issues?
- Who sets the policy agenda?
  In setting the agenda, what is role of [cabinet? FRELIMO? *(Moz.)*/civil servants? Politicians? *(Nig.)*/cabinet? National Resistance Movement? *(Ug.)*] Ministry of Finance? Donors?

Nutrition within the policy arena in [Mozambique/ Nigeria/Uganda]

- [The PARPA and PROAGRI/The principal development policy documents for Nigeria/The PEAP and the PMA] do not address nutrition in detail. For example, nutritional status is not one of the benchmarks in the [PARPA/*(this sentence not in Nigeria guide)*/PEAP] by which progress in eradicating poverty will be measured. In your view, is this a significant omission?
  - Overall, is nutrition a pressing policy issue in [Mozambique/Nigeria/ Uganda]? Is the government subject to criticism for lack of attention to nutrition policies and programmes?
  - If not, assess the validity of the perspective that says that if [Mozambicans/Nigerians/Ugandans] can foster sustained economic growth, any nutritional problems will take care of themselves?
- If someone talks about "nutrition policy" for [Mozambique/Nigeria/ Uganda], what comes to mind?
  - Are you aware of any government statements on food and nutrition policy? If so, how important are these in guiding government action and resource allocation?
  - Who do you perceive to be the primary beneficiaries of nutrition policy debates?
- Similarly, what do you assume a "nutrition programme" would consist of in [Mozambique/Nigeria/Uganda]? Who would be targeted? What ministries would be involved? What would be the programme content?

Nutrition within government activities

- What are the costs associated with formulating and implementing nutrition policy and interventions? Consider scarce human resources and organizational constraints, as well as financial constraints.

- In the past, has nutrition had a higher profile in government policy and action than today?
  - If so, when and why? What was the content of these earlier activities? How effective were they? Were these policies explicitly reversed?

Decentralization (*Uganda only*)

- With decentralization, do hungry or malnourished people have a louder voice in Ugandan political debate? Does decentralization make any difference for them?
  - What organizations provide such a voice by calling attention to the malnourished and advocating for effective nutrition interventions? How effective are these organizations?
- Are there local government authorities that have nutrition and household food security as action points on their district plans?
- Is there any funding mechanism from central government to the districts that is linked to nutritional activities and outcomes?
  - If not, how could such activities be supported at the district and subdistrict level?

Agriculturalists and nutritionists working together

- In closing, to return to the overarching aim of this study, do you have any additional insights into how agriculturalists and nutritionists conduct their activities in [Mozambique/Nigeria/ Uganda], whether jointly or separately?
  - What linkages between the two communities that already exist could be strengthened to improve the condition of malnourished [Mozambicans/ Nigerians/Ugandans]?
  - What opportunities exist that are currently not being exploited?

APPENDIX C

Sample Interview Guide for Institutional Study in Ghana

This guide was used during the interviews conducted for the institutional study of agriculture and nutrition for the TANA project during fieldwork in Ghana in March 2004. It was developed by modifying the guide (presented in Appendix B) that had been used for fieldwork in the other three country studies that was done in late 2002. When the request was made to extend the institutional study to Ghana, the opportunity was taken to modify the interview guide to cover gaps found in the earlier studies and to follow up in more detail on unexpected issues that emerged in the other three countries.

Introductory statement made to interviewee

The problem statement underlying the study is as follows:

The agriculture and nutrition communities are missing opportunities to more effectively reduce poverty, hunger, and malnutrition by failing to combine scarce resources, act together and, in part, to adequately incorporate gender analysis throughout their work.

This study is to examine how the agriculture and nutrition communities interact in Ghana and the policy processes fostering or constraining their interaction. The study will examine

- where agriculture and nutrition are located within the institutional arrangement of government at the national, state, and local government authority levels;
- the professional formation and working conditions of agriculturalists and nutritionists and how these factors are reflected in their level of collaboration;
- how policies are made in Ghana and the priority accorded to agriculture and nutrition; and
- the importance of nutrition in the formulation and implementation of the national development plans, sectoral public expenditure plans for agriculture, and national food and nutrition strategies.

Underlying this study is the assertion that the social process through which agriculture and nutrition are linked—how food gets on the table and eaten—has an inherent gender element. Consequently, the study will explicitly examine the use made of gender analyses both in designing policies and in formulating activities that aim to improve the nutrition of Ghanaians.

Two principal methods will be used—a close review of the literature on Ghanaian government policy, agriculture, and nutrition, and interviews with key informants in Ghana. This questionnaire is to serve the latter method.

The key informants will be government policy makers, particularly those linked to the Food and Nutrition Security Network, as well as agriculturalists and nutritionists in government; academics in the fields of nutrition and agricultural research; the staff of nongovernmental organizations working in the area of food security, nutrition, and agriculture; and donors supporting such efforts in Ghana. Most interviews will be carried out in Accra.

Information on the respondent

- Position; Age; Sex; Training (incl. gender analysis); Career path; Likely future career path.
- Does your position involve agriculture, nutrition, and linkages between them? If so, how?
- Is gender or, alternatively, an understanding of the roles, activities, and responsibilities of men and women an important component of the work you do?
    - Have you made use of gender analyses in planning your activities?
    - Have you made use of community studies in planning that included information on the needs/roles of men and women? If so, how did you use such information?
- Individual's place within organogram of agriculture and nutrition institutions (formal/informal).

Nutritional status of Ghana's population

- Is malnutrition perceived to be a problem in Ghana in general—whether hunger, insufficient calories or protein, or micronutrient deficiencies?
    - If yes, describe the problem.
    - If no, would you give an assessment of how much this is due to conscious government policy and how much to Ghana being well endowed for productive agriculture?

- What about if you look at the provincial or district level?
- What about within the population? Are there similarities/dissimilarities in the way this problem affects men and women, girls and boys in Ghana (better/worse, different)?
- If there are differences within the population, what might different government institutions do to respond to those? (*Probe for the various government agencies*)
- How effective are these institutions? Why? (*Probe for issues related to capacity, institutional organization, political attention to gender issues, resource priorities, etc.*)
- What institution(s) in government do you believe is/are responsible for the nutritional well-being of the population? Why?
    - Why not agriculture, health, local government, Women & Children's Affairs (*delete as needed*)?
- How do you find out about the nutritional status of Ghanaians?
    - What about differences between men and women, boys and girls? How available is this information?

Relationship between professionals in relevant fields in Ghana

- What are the central objectives of agriculturalist in their professional activities?
    - How about for nutritionists?
- How would you characterize the professional relationship between nutritionists and agriculturalists in Ghana?
    - What about that between health professionals and nutritionists?
    - Between gender specialists and agriculturalists? Nutritionists and gender specialists?
- What advantages or disadvantages might there be to greater cooperation between agriculturalists and nutritionists?

- Could or should they work together more closely? Benefits/costs of doing so?
- How much interaction do you have with specialists in the other field? Did you receive training with them? Attend workshops together?
  - If you look at the interactions between agriculturalists and nutritionists at national, district, and community levels, is the quality of the interactions of the two groups similar, regardless of the level at which they work?
  - Why is this the case? Are there any incentives (disincentives) in place at certain levels to encourage (impede) collaboration?
- Do any examples of successful nutrition programs that link agriculturalists with nutritionists come to mind?
  - Was gender analysis used in any way in the design of these programs?
- It is suggested that if we focus attention on people, that is, men and women, girls and boys (their activities, needs, and available resources), versus technologies or service delivery mechanisms, we might find new ways to implement interventions that strengthen the links between agriculture and nutrition. Would you agree or disagree with that? Explain. (*May need an example*)
  - Does decentralization provide a better opportunity to adopt a people-centered approach or a technologies approach?
- In the formulation of government budgets, do nutritionists and agriculturalists tend to compete for the same funds or do they work in concert to get a larger slice of the budget for agriculture, food, and nutrition activities? Explain why this is so.
- This study assumes that linking nutrition and agriculture is a timely and more effective way to meet hunger and malnutrition challenges. Consequently, we promote the idea that policies and programmes should foster nutritionists and agriculturists working more closely together. What is your assessment of this perspective?

Gender policy, agriculture, and nutrition in Ghana

- How central are gender considerations to how Ghanaian agriculturalists work? Why? (Probe with understanding/responding to the different needs, roles/activities, resources of men and women)
  - How central are gender considerations to how Ghanaian nutritionists work? Why?
- In general, how would you assess your colleagues' gender capacity in the nutrition field? In agriculture? (*Probe about their level of understanding of gender [or alternate wording], ability to use gender tools, etc.*)
- In your institution, is there a gender focal point (e.g., person/office who attends to different needs of women and men in nutrition/agriculture, offers expertise in gender analysis or training)? (*Can refer to organogram*)
  - How diffuse is this expertise (cross-cutting the institution or concentrated in one office)?
  - Does this focal point provide input into nutrition or agricultural policies? Provide input into the institution's work? Describe.
  - Does this focal point interact with professionals in nutrition or agriculture (whichever is the "other" field)?
- Are there bodies (groups, committees, government agencies) that work to integrate gender into nutrition policies and activities? Into agricultural policies and activities?
  - In general, how effective are they? (*Probe for examples*)
  - Do government authorities at national, district, and community

levels all have equivalent under-standing and capacity to address the gender aspects of nutritional prob-lems? Or are there differences de-pending on scale?

- This study assumes that gender is a critical aspect of the process by which improved food production leads to bet-ter nutrition. Consequently, we promote the idea that gender should be a central component in the design and imple-mentation of nutrition policies and pro-grammes. What is your assessment of this perspective?
  - (*If need to probe:*) Does this per-spective state the obvious and so is meaningless? Or it is an uncom-mon, but important perspective? Or is it only one of several impor-tant aspects?

Policy making in Ghana

- Could you describe how policy deci-sions are made in government?
  - Is this pattern seen at both national and regional and district levels? If not, what are the differences?
- What are the basic motivations for most politicians taking action on policy issues?
- Who sets the policy agenda?
  - In setting the agenda, what is role of technical civil servants? Politicians? Ministry of Finance? Donors?
- Are there particular agricultural (or nu-trition) policies that you find especially relevant to your work as a nutritionist (or agriculturalist)? How so? (*Modify question based on whether the respon-dent is a nutritionist or agriculturalist. Probe for specific policies in the "other" field.*)
- How adequately would you say gender issues have been incorporated into nutri-tion or agricultural policies or debates?
  - Which policies do this well? Which do not?
  - Have some gender issues been incorporated in such policy while

others have not? What is missing? Why do you think some aspects are missing?

- Gender is said to be less visible and less well understood when talking about policies, and more visible and well understood when talking about community- and household-level inter-ventions. What do you think about this?
  - [*Assessment of notion that people "get" gender when talking about a farmer but not when talking about taxation or other broader issues that impact on agricultural produc-tion and the way production activi-ties are defined by gender.*]
  - How might that affect how eco-nomic or fiscal policies impact on men and women?

Nutrition within the policy arena in Ghana

- The principal development policy doc-uments for Ghana do not address nutri-tion in detail. In your view, is this a sig-nificant omission?
  - Overall, is nutrition a pressing pol-icy issue in Ghana? Is the govern-ment subject to criticism for lack of attention to nutrition policies and programmes?
  - If not, assess the validity of the per-spective that says that if Ghanaians can foster sustained economic growth, any nutritional problems will take care of themselves?
- If someone talks about "nutrition pol-icy" for Ghana, what comes to mind?
  - Are you aware of any government statements on food and nutrition policy? If so, how important are these in guiding government action and resource allocation?
  - Who do you perceive to be the pri-mary beneficiaries of any nutrition policy debates?
  - What about for major agricultural policies?

- How well were the gender aspects of these policies implemented? Why?
- Similarly, what do you assume a "nutrition programme" would consist of in Ghana?
    - Who would be targeted? Ministries involved? Programme content?
    - What are the costs associated with implementing nutrition policy and interventions? Consider scarce human resources, organizational and financial constraints.
- In the past, has nutrition had a higher profile in government policy and action than today?
    - If so, when and why? What was the content of these earlier activities? How effective were they? Were these policies explicitly reversed?

- How well were the gender aspects of these policies implemented? Why?

Agriculturalists and nutritionists working together

- In closing, to return to the overarching aim of this study, do you have any additional insights into how agriculturalists and nutritionists conduct their activities in Ghana, whether jointly or separately?
- What linkages between the two communities that already exist could be strengthened to improve the condition of malnourished Ghanaians?
    - What opportunities exist that are currently not being exploited?

References

ACC/SCN-IFPRI (United Nations Administrative Committee on Coordination, Standing Committee on Nutrition–International Food Policy Research Institute). 2000. *Fourth report on the world nutrition situation.* Geneva: ACC/SCN in collaboration with IFPRI.

Alderman, H., J. Hoddinott, and B. Kinsey. 2003. *Long term consequences of early childhood malnutrition.* Food Consumption and Nutrition Division Discussion Paper 168. Washington, D.C.: International Food Policy Research Institute.

Appiah, F., J. A. Ayee, J. Appeah, K. Baah-Wiredu, R. Martin, J. Steffensen, and S. Trollegaard. 2000. *Fiscal decentralisation and sub-national government finance in relation to infrastructure and service provision in Ghana.* Fiscal Decentralisation and Sub-national Finance in Africa Series. Washington, D.C.: World Bank.

Behrman, J., H. Alderman, and J. Hoddinott. 2004. Hunger and malnutrition. In *Global crises, global solutions,* ed. B. Lomborg. Cambridge: Cambridge University Press.

Benson, T., T. Palmer, R. Satcher, and C. Johnson-Welch. 2004. *Crossing boundaries to reduce malnutrition? An institutional study of agriculture and nutrition in Uganda, Mozambique, Nigeria, and Ghana.* Report submitted to International Center for Research on Women under the Agriculture–Nutrition Advantage project. Washington, D.C.: International Food Policy Research Institute.

Christiaensen, L., and H. Alderman. 2004. Child malnutrition in Ethiopia: Can maternal knowledge augment the role of income? *Economic Development and Cultural Change* 52 (2): 287–312.

Clark, T. W. 2002. *The policy process—A practical guide for natural resource professionals.* New Haven, Conn., U.S.A.: Yale University Press.

Crewe, E., and J. Young. 2002. *Bridging research and policy: Context, evidence, and links.* Overseas Development Institute (ODI) Working Paper 173. London: ODI.

de Haan, A. 2002. Nutrition in Poverty Reduction Strategy Papers: What role for "social issues" in the new aid architecture? Background paper for the Fifth Report on the World Nutrition Situation. Geneva: United Nations Administrative Committee on Coordination, Sub-Committee on Nutrition (ACC/SCN).

deLeon, P. 1999. The stages approach to the policy process. In *Theories of the policy process,* ed. P. A. Sabatier. Boulder, Colo. U.S.A.: Westview Press.

Ethiopian PROFILES Team and AED/Linkages. 2005. Why nutrition matters. Presentation on the Ethiopian PROFILES analysis. Addis Ababa: AED/Linkages.

Ezzati, M., A. D. Lopez, A. Rodgers, S. Vander Hoorn, C. J. L. Murray, and the Comparative Risk Assessment Collaborating Group. 2003. Selected major risk factors and global and regional burden of disease. *Lancet* 360: 1347–1360.

FAO (Food and Agriculture Organization of the United Nations). 2005. *The state of food insecurity in the world, 2005.* Rome.

———. 2006. FAOStat—FAO statistical databases. On-line agricultural and food databases and extraction tool. http://apps.fao.org/.

Filmer, D. 2005. Educational attainment and enrollment around the world. On-line database and data extraction tool. Development Research Group, World Bank. http://www.worldbank.org/research/projects/edattain/edattain.htm.

FIVIMS/FAO (Food Insecurity and Vulnerability Information and Mapping System/Food and Agriculture Organization of the United Nations). 2002. Measurement and assessment of food deprivation and undernutrition. Summary of proceedings of an international scientific symposium convened by the Agriculture and Economic Development Analysis Division, FAO, June 26–28, Rome.

Gillespie, S., M. McLachlan, and R. Shrimpton, eds. 2003. *Combating malnutrition: Time to act.* Washington, D.C.: World Bank.

GOG (Government of Ghana). 1995. *Ghana National Plan of Action on Food and Nutrition—1995–2000.* Accra.

———. 2003. *Ghana Poverty Reduction Strategy—2003–2005: An agenda for growth and prosperity.* Accra: National Development Planning Commission.

Grindle, M. S. 2004. *Despite the odds: The contentious politics of education reform.* Princeton, N.J., U.S.A.: Princeton University Press.

Grindle, M. S., and J. W. Thomas. 1989. Policy makers, policy choices, and policy outcomes: The political economy of reform in developing countries. *Policy Sciences* 22: 213–248.

———. 1991. *Public choice and policy change: The political economy of reform in developing countries.* Baltimore: Johns Hopkins University Press.

Haddad, L., H. Alderman, S. Appleton, L. Song, and Y. Yohannes. 2003. Reducing child malnutrition: How far does income growth take us? *World Bank Economic Review* 17: 107–131.

Hajer, M. A. 1995. *The politics of environmental discourse: Ecological modernization and the policy process.* Oxford: Clarendon Press.

Heaver, R. 2002. *Improving nutrition—Issues in management and capacity development.* Health, Nutrition, and Population Discussion Paper. Washington, D.C.: World Bank.

Henry, G. T. 1990. *Practical sampling.* Applied Social Research Methods Series 21. Newbury Park, Calif., U.S.A.: Sage Publications.

Horowitz, D. L. 1989. Is there a third-world policy process? *Policy Sciences* 22: 197–212.

HTF (Hunger Task Force). 2003. *Halving hunger by 2015: A framework for action.* Interim report of the Millennium Project. New York: United Nations Development Programme.

ICRW/IFPRI (International Center for Research on Women/International Food Policy Research Institute). 2004. *The agriculture–nutrition advantage—Picking up the pace in the fight against hunger.* Washington, D.C.: ICRW.

Jenkins-Smith, H. C., and P. A. Sabatier. 1993. The study of public policy processes. In *Policy change and learning: An advocacy coalition approach,* ed. P. A. Sabatier and H. C. Jenkins-Smith. Boulder, Colo., U.S.A.: Westview Press.

Johnson-Welch, C., K. MacQuarrie, and S. Bunch. 2005. *Promoting the agriculture–nutrition advantage—A leadership strategy to reducing hunger and malnutrition in Africa.* Washington, D.C.: International Center for Research on Women.

Jonsson, U. 1993. Integrating political and economic factors within nutrition-related policy research: An economic perspective. In *The political economy of food and nutrition policies,* ed. P. Pinstrup-Andersen. Baltimore: Johns Hopkins University Press.

Kaufmann, D., A. Kraay, and M. Mastruzzi. 2006. *Governance matters V: Governance indicators for 1996–2004.* Washington, D.C.: World Bank.

Kaufmann, D., A. Kraay, and P. Zoido-Lobatón. 2002. *Governance matters II: Updated indicators for 2000/01.* World Bank Policy Research Working Paper 2772. Washington, D.C.: World Bank.

Keeley, J., and I. Scoones. 1999. *Understanding environmental policy processes: A review.* Institute of Development Studies (IDS) Working Paper 89. Brighton, UK: IDS, University of Sussex.

———. 2003. *Understanding environmental policy processes—Cases from Africa.* London: Earthscan Publications.

Kingdon, J. W. 1995. *Agendas, alternatives and public policies.* Second edition. New York: Harper-Collins.

Kurz, K., and C. Johnson-Welch. 2001. Enhancing women's contribution to improving food consumption and nutrition. *Food and Nutrition Bulletin* 22 (4): 443–453.

Levin, C., J. Long, K. R. Simler, and C. Johnson-Welch. 2003. *Cultivating nutrition: A survey of opinions on integrating agriculture and nutrition.* Food Consumption and Nutrition Division Discussion Paper 154. Washington, D.C.: International Food Policy Research Institute.

Levinson, J. 2000. Searching for a home: The institutionalization issue in international nutrition. Paper prepared for assessment workshop of World Bank and UNICEF on nutrition policy and practice at global and country levels, January 18–20, Washington, D.C. Mimeo.

MAAIF and MFPED (Ministry of Agriculture, Animal Industry, and Fisheries and Ministry of Finance, Planning and Economic Development). 2000. *Plan of Modernisation of Agriculture: Eradicating poverty in Uganda (government strategy and operational framework).* Kampala.

MAAIF and MOH (Ministry of Agriculture, Animal Industry, and Fisheries and Ministry of Health). 2003. *Uganda food and nutrition policy.* Kampala.

———. 2005. *Uganda food and nutrition strategy.* Kampala.

Mason, J. B. 2000. How nutrition improves and what that implies for policy decisions. Paper prepared for World Bank and UNICEF assessment workshop on nutrition policy and practice at global and country levels, January 18–20, Washington, D.C. Mimeo.

MFPED (Ministry of Finance, Planning, and Economic Development). 2000. *Uganda's poverty eradication action plan—Summary and main objectives.* Kampala.

———. 2005. *Poverty eradication action plan (2004/5–2007/8).* Kampala.

MOFA (Ministry of Food and Agriculture). 2002. *Food and agriculture sector development policy (FASDEP).* Accra.

Neilson, S. 2001. *IDRC and its influence on public policy. Knowledge utilization and public policy processes: A literature review.* Ottawa: International Development Research Centre Evaluation Unit.

NPC (National Planning Commission). 2001. *National policy on food and nutrition in Nigeria.* Abuja, Nigeria.

———. 2003. *National plan of action on food and nutrition in Nigeria.* Abuja, Nigeria.

———. 2004. *National economic empowerment and development strategy.* Abuja, Nigeria.

ORC (Opinion Research Corporation)/Macro. 2007. *Demographic and Health Surveys STATcompiler.* On-line Demographic and Health Survey data extraction tool. http://www.measuredhs.com/start.cfm.

Oxford University Press. 2002. Oxford English dictionary. Second edition. Online edition. http://dictionary.oed.com/.

Paarlberg, R. 2002. *Governance and food security in an age of globalization.* 2020 Vision for Food, Agriculture, and the Environment Discussion Paper 36. Washington, D.C.: International Food Policy Research Institute.

Population Reference Bureau. 2006. 2006 World population data sheet. On-line database. http://www.prb.org/pdf06/06WorldDataSheet.pdf.

Porter, R. D., with I. Hicks. 1994. Knowledge utilization and the process of policy formation: Toward a framework for Africa. Paper prepared for the Support for Analysis and Research in Africa

(SARA) Project, U.S. Agency for International Development. http://www.dec.org/pdf_docs/PNABX317.pdf.

Ramakrishnan, U., R. Martorell, D. Schroeder, and R. Flores. 1999. Intergenerational effects on linear growth. *Journal of Nutrition* 129 (2): 544–549.

Ranis, G., F. Stewart, and A. Ramirez. 2000. Economic growth and human development. *World Development* 28 (2): 197–219.

Republic of Mozambique. 2001. *Action plan for the reduction of absolute poverty (2001–2005) (PARPA)—Strategy document for the reduction of poverty and promotion of economic growth.* Maputo: Republic of Mozambique. (Translated from Portuguese).

Rokx, C. 2000. *Who should implement nutrition interventions?—The application of institutional economics to nutrition and the significance of various constraints to the implementation of nutrition interventions.* Health, Nutrition, and Population Discussion Paper. Washington, D.C.: World Bank.

Sabatier, P. A. 1993. Policy change over a decade or more. In *Policy change and learning: An advocacy coalition approach,* ed. P. A. Sabatier and H. C. Jenkins-Smith. Boulder, Colo., U.S.A.: Westview Press.

Sabatier, P. A., and H. C. Jenkins-Smith. 1999. The advocacy coalition framework: An assessment. In *Theories of the policy process,* ed. P. A. Sabatier. Boulder, Colo., U.S.A.: Westview Press.

Sen, A. 1999. *Development as freedom.* Oxford: Oxford University Press.

Shrimpton, R. 2002. A strategic plan for nutrition in Mozambique. Maputo: Nutrition Section, Ministry of Health. Mimeo.

Shrimpton, R., C. G. Victora, M. de Onis, R. Costa Lima, M. Blössner, and G. Clugston. 2001. Worldwide timing of growth faltering: Implications for nutritional interventions. *Pediatrics* 107 (5): e75.

Smith, L., and L. Haddad. 2000. *Explaining child malnutrition in developing countries: A cross-country analysis.* IFPRI Research Report 111. Washington, D.C.: International Food Policy Research Institute.

Stone, D. 2001. Getting research into policy? Paper presented at the third Global Development Network conference, December 10, Rio de Janeiro. http://www.gdnet.org/rapnet/pdf/ Beyond%20Economics%20Stone.pdf.

Stone, D., S. Maxwell, and M. Keating. 2001. Bridging research and policy. Paper presented at an international workshop funded by the U.K. Department for International Development, July 16–17, Warwick University, Warwick.

Townsend, M. S., J. Peerson, B. Love, C. Achterberg, and S. P. Murphy. 2001. Food insecurity is positively related to overweight in women. *Journal of Nutrition* 131: 1738–1745.

UNDP (United Nations Development Programme). 1993. *Human development report 1993: Peoples' participation.* New York: UNDP and Oxford University Press.

———. 2006. Human development indicators 2006. On-line database and data extraction tool. http://hdr.undp.org/.

UNICEF (United Nations Children's Fund). 1990. *Strategy for improved nutrition of children and women in developing countries. A UNICEF policy review.* New York.

———. 2005. The state of the world's children 2005. Online database. http://www.unicef.org/sowc05/english/statistics.html.

United Nations General Assembly. 1948. *Universal Declaration of Human Rights.* General Assembly resolution 217A (III), UN Document A/810 at 71.

———. 1966. *International Covenant of Economic, Social, and Cultural Rights.* 21 General Assembly resolution 2220A (XXI), supp. (no. 16) at 49.

———. 1989. *Convention on the Rights of the Child.* 44 General Assembly resolution 44/25, annex, supp. (no. 49) at 167.

Weiss, C. 1977. Research for policy's sake: The enlightenment function of social science research. *Policy Analysis* 3 (4): 531–545.

Williamson, O. E. 1999. Public and private bureaucracies: A transaction cost economics perspective. *Journal of Law, Economics, and Organization* 15 (1): 306–342.

World Bank. 2003. *World development report 2003: Sustainable development in a dynamic world.* Washington, D.C., and New York: World Bank and Oxford University Press.

———. 2006a. *Repositioning nutrition as central to development: A strategy for large-scale action.* Washington, D.C.: World Bank.

———. 2006b. The 2006 world development indicators. Washington, D.C.: Development Data Group, World Bank. CD-ROM.

Zahariadis, N. 1999. Ambiguity, time, and multiple streams. In *Theories of the policy process,* ed. P. A. Sabatier. Boulder, Colo., U.S.A.: Westview Press.